Bloom's Modern Critical Interpretations

George Orwell's
Animal Farm
New Edition

Edited and with an introduction by
Harold Bloom
Sterling Professor of the Humanities
Yale University

BLOOM'S
LITERARY CRITICISM
An imprint of Infobase Publishing

Bloom's Modern Critical Interpretations:
Animal Farm—New Edition

Copyright © 2009 by Infobase Publishing

Introduction © 2009 by Harold Bloom

Bloom's Literary Criticism
An imprint of Infobase Publishing
132 West 31st Street
New York NY 10001

Library of Congress Cataloging-in-Publication Data
George Orwell's Animal farm / edited and with an introduction by Harold Bloom.
— New ed.
    p. cm. — (Bloom's modern critical interpretations)
  Includes bibliographical references and index.
  ISBN 978-1-60413-582-4 (acid-free paper)
  1. Orwell, George, 1903–1950. Animal farm.   2. Political fiction, English—History and criticism. 3.   Satire, English—History and criticism.   4. Dystopias in literature.
  I. Bloom, Harold.   II. Title.   III. Series.
  PR6029.R8A746 2010
  823'.912—dc22   2009018851

Contributing editor: Pamela Loos
Cover designed by Takeshi Takahashi

Printed in the United States of America
IBT IBT 10 9 8 7 6 5 4 3 2 1

This book is printed on acid-free paper.

Contents

Editor's Note

My introduction grants that *Animal Farm* remains relevant, because the dangers of a computerized society carry on from Orwell's horror of Stalinist terror, even though I find the book less than an aesthetic achievement, since a beast fable needs a psychological clarity that is lacking here.

Daphne Patai offers a feminist critique of *Animal Farm* that does not persuade me, but then I am seventy-nine and resistant to ideologues, as in fact Orwell was.

Valerie Meyers sensibly unravels the allegorical thread of the beast fable, while Samir Elbarbary follows Orwell in his concern for language mystification in politics.

Orwell's continued belief in a democratic socialism is argued by V.C. Letemendia, though I myself read *Animal Farm* as despairing of all politics.

Roger Fowler interprets *Animal Farm* as an allegory of the falsification of history by politics, after which Roger Pearce demonstrates Tolstoy's influence on the book.

The fable is seen as a parable of the self-destruction of human decency by Anthony Stewart, while Peter Edgerly Firchow traces the transition from *Animal Farm* to *Nineteen Eighty-Four*.

HAROLD BLOOM

Introduction

One critic remarked of George Orwell that he wrote sympathetically about human beings only when he presented them as animals. The truth of this can be tested by comparing *Animal Farm* to *Nineteen Eighty-Four*; Napoleon (Stalin) is preferable to the torturer O'Brien, perhaps because even a whip-wielding boar is more tolerated by Orwell than a sadistic human. Poor Boxer, the martyred workhorse, is certainly more lovable than Winston Smith, and Mollie the flirtatious mare is more charming than poor Julia. Orwell's dislike of people resembles that of a much greater moral satirist, Jonathan Swift: Each loved individual persons, while despising mankind in the mass. Whatever the aesthetic flaws of *Animal Farm*, it seems to me a better book than *Nineteen Eighty-Four*, primarily because it allows us a few animals with whom we can identify. Even Benjamin, the ill-tempered old donkey, silent and cynical, and incapable of laughing, still becomes somewhat dear to us, largely because of his devotion to the heroic Boxer. I'm not certain that I don't prefer Snowball (Trotsky) to anyone at all in *Nineteen Eighty-Four*, because at least he is vivacious and inventive.

The great Canadian critic Northrop Frye observed that *Animal Farm* adapts from Swift's *A Tale of a Tub* the classical formula of much literary satire: "the corruption of principle by expediency," or the fall of Utopia. Unlike Swift, however, as Frye again notes, Orwell is not concerned with motivation. The reader is not encouraged to ask: What does the inscrutable Napoleon-Stalin want? Orwell's point may be that absolute power is desired by tyrants simply for its own sake, but *Animal Farm* hardly makes that very clear. The beast fable is a fascinating genre, but it demands a certain psychological clarity, whether in Chaucer or in Thurber, and *Animal Farm* mostly evades psychological categories.

Orwell essentially was a liberal moralist, grimly preoccupied with preserving a few old-fashioned virtues while fearing that the technological future would only enhance human depravity. *Animal Farm*, like *Nineteen Eighty-Four*, retains its relevance because we are entering into a computerized world where a post-Orwellian "virtual reality" could be used as yet another betrayal of individual liberty. Part of the residual strength of *Animal Farm* is that we can imagine a version of it in early twenty-first-century America in which all the "animals" will be compelled to live some variant upon a theocratic "Contract with the American Family." Perhaps the motto of that theocracy will be: "All animals are holy, but some animals are holier than others."

DAPHNE PATAI

Political Fiction and Patriarchal Fantasy

In his essay "Marrakech," Orwell elaborates on the perception that came to him, during his stay in Morocco, that "All people who work with their hands are partly invisible." Describing the file of "very old women," each bent beneath a load of firewood, who passed by his house every afternoon for several weeks, he comments: "I cannot truly say that I had seen them. Firewood was passing—that was how I saw it" (CEJL, 1:391). One day he happened to be walking behind the firewood and finally noticed "the human being underneath it"—a woman. By contrast, he writes, his awareness of the mistreatment of animals was immediate: "I had not been five minutes on Moroccan soil before I noticed the overloading of the donkeys and was infuriated by it." Orwell then describes the small Moroccan donkey, a faithful and willing worker, in the anthropomorphic terms he was later to use for Boxer, the immense and hardworking cart horse in *Animal Farm*, and concludes: "After a dozen years of devoted work, it suddenly drops dead, whereupon its master tips it into the ditch and the village dogs have torn its guts out before it is cold" (1:392). In a fascinating example of his tendency to generalize from personal reactions, Orwell states: "This kind of thing makes one's blood boil, whereas—on the whole—the plight of the human beings does not. I am not commenting, merely pointing to a fact. People with brown skins are next door to invisible. Anyone can be sorry for the donkey

From *The Orwell Mystique: A Study in Male Ideology*, pp. 201–18, 306–10. © 1984 by Daphne Patai.

3

with its galled back, but it is generally owing to some kind of accident if one even notices the old woman under her load of sticks" (1:392). The woman, Orwell had earlier explained, "accepted her status as an old woman, that is to say as a beast of burden" (1:391). Rebellion is not a possibility for her, any more than for the Negro soldiers (very visible to Orwell, however) described later in the same essay as unaware of their potential power.

Orwell explained the genesis of *Animal Farm* in a 1947 preface to the Ukrainian edition of the book. For a decade he had "been convinced that the destruction of the Soviet myth was essential if we wanted a revival of the Socialist movement."

> On my return from Spain I thought of exposing the Soviet myth in a story that could be easily understood by almost anyone and which could be easily translated into other languages. However the actual details of the story did not come to me for some time until one day (I was then living in a small village) I saw a little boy, perhaps ten years old, driving a huge cart-horse along a narrow path, whipping it whenever it tried to turn. It struck me that if only such animals became aware of their strength we should have no power over them, and that men exploit animals in much the same way as the rich exploit the proletariat.
>
> I proceeded to analyse Marx's theory from the animals' point of view. To them it was clear that the concept of a class struggle between humans was pure illusion, since whenever it was necessary to exploit animals, all humans united against them: the true struggle is between animals and humans. From this point of departure, it was not difficult to elaborate the story. [CEJL, 3:405–6]

In Morocco, Orwell perceived the cruel labor of donkeys more readily than that of brown-skinned women. Though he abstracts himself from his description and attributes his reaction to all people ("merely pointing to a fact"), this is a characteristic perception for Orwell. We see it duplicated in his account of how he came to write *Animal Farm*. For when Orwell was ready to think in terms of exploitation that transcends economic class, he blindly leaped from class to species without pausing to consider the question of gender. It was apparently easier for Orwell to identify with the animal kingdom, exploited at the hands of "humans," than to note that buried in class and race divisions in the human world lay the issue of gender oppression.

The animals' perspective adopted by Orwell as the starting point for his fable leads him to a conclusion—that the class struggle among humans is "pure illusion"—which is itself an illusion. Although humans have been united in their exploitation of animals, this does not mean that they are united in all other respects. There can exist both a class struggle and a general exploitation of animals. Only this gross simplification, however, enabled Orwell to write *Animal Farm*; in fact, the choice of allegory allowed Orwell to turn his penchant for generalization, one of his fundamental weaknesses as a writer, into a strength, for, as Gay Clifford points out, "allegory invites its readers ... to see the particular narrative as being also a series of generalized statements, and demands that concepts be identified simultaneously in their fictional and ideological roles."[1] Clifford goes on to state that both *Animal Farm* and *Nineteen Eighty-Four*, like other modern allegories, "require a single act of translation (fiction to history for example) and then can be read as straight narratives whose moral significance is obvious. Indeed, without that clearly delimited act of translation they lose half their force."[2]

Allegory, like myth, presupposes an audience that will respond in certain ways.[3] This is one reason, Northrop Frye has observed, that critics dislike allegory, for it restricts the freedom of their commentary by prescribing its direction.[4] In Clifford's words: "The idea that there are as many ways of reading a work of literature as there are readers is anathema to allegory."[5] This observation is borne out by Orwell's anxious concern that *Animal Farm* be read "correctly." After the manuscript's rejection by Dial Press in New York in 1944, on the grounds that "it was impossible to sell animal stories in the USA," Orwell was "not sure whether one can count on the American public grasping what it is about," as he explained in a letter to his agent (CEJL, 4:110); and he even suggested that "it might be worth indicating on the dust-jacket of the American edition what the book is about" (4:111). Orwell need not have worried. When published in the United States in 1946, *Animal Farm* was the Book-of-the-Month Club main selection, and an unprecedented special letter was sent by the club's president to its members urging them to choose *Animal Farm* rather than an alternative title. It sold over half a million copies (4:519) in the club edition alone. Far from not being understood, it was immediately put to work as an anti-Communist text and to this day is taught in American schools, apparently for this purpose.[6]

Patriarch Pigs, Maternal Mares, and Other Animals

The psychological appeal of the animal fable is easy to understand: By projecting human conflicts onto animal characters, readers can avoid feeling threatened or overwhelmed by the real-world problems they encounter in this simplified and in many respects charming form.[7] Neither the author nor the readers, however, are magically freed from their own prejudices by this displacement. On the contrary, a fable such as *Animal Farm* relies considerably upon engaging the reader's preconceived ideas. The author's particular concerns can be more clearly set in relief against a background of familiar and nonchallenging elements. In his fable, Orwell evokes not only our sympathy for certain animals but also our possible distaste for pigs, fear of barking and biting dogs, and awe at the size and strength of horses. But even in the early stages of his story he does not merely portray the animals as united in their animalness against the species *Homo sapiens*; nor, as the story develops, does he simply elicit "anti" feelings for the pigs and "pro" feelings for the other animals without further distinctions.

To be effective, an animal fable must maintain a delicate balance between the evocation of the animals' human characteristics and their recognizable animal traits. The reader must use both perspectives, the human and the animal, simultaneously, if the allegory is not to become ludicrous.[8] Orwell provides a poignantly humorous example of this in describing how the animals went through the farmhouse after the revolution: "Some hams hanging in the kitchen were taken out for burial" (22). Even Snowball's writing down of the Seven Commandments of Animalism is endearing: "It was very neatly written, and except that 'friend' was written 'freind' and one of the 'S's' was the wrong way round, the spelling was correct all the way through" (23). Descriptions such as this occur at many points in the text, and their emotional appeal clearly comes from the childlike quality of the details. At this stage of the proceedings the reader sees nothing sinister in the pigs' new-found literacy. Again and again Orwell attributes childlike tastes and habits to the animals, their love of singing their anthem, "Beasts of England," many times over, for example. This feature also explains why the book can be read with pleasure by children, who no doubt identify more intensely than adults with the animals and their lack of total command of adult human skills. At the same time, the flattened characterizations suitable for animal allegory neutralize some of Orwell's special difficulties as a writer of fiction. He has at last found a framework in which authentic relationships between characters and insight into human beings—ordinary requirements of the novel—are simply not important.

Orwell's animal challenge to Marxism presupposes a unity among the animals (as among the humans) that is purely imaginary. Katharine Burdekin, in an extraordinary feminist novel entitled *Proud Man*, published in 1934 under the pseudonym "Murray Constantine," depicts British society from the vantage point of an evolved self-fertilizing "person" who refers to the rest of us as "subhumans." Burdekin's narrator states the matter in plain language: "A privilege of class divides a subhuman society horizontally, while a privilege of sex divides it vertically."[9] Burdekin also discusses the problem of failed revolutions (which was later to preoccupy Orwell) and labels them "reversals of privilege." She relates these to the human preoccupation with the idea of importance, exacerbated in males due to their biological limitations—"womb envy," in short.[10] In *Animal Farm*, however, Orwell does not address the vertical division of society—by sex—on which patriarchy rests. Of course, we know that his aim was to satirize "dictatorship in general"[11] and the Russian Revolution in particular; but displacing his political message onto animals did not allow Orwell an avenue of escape from the messy business of the gender hierarchy. On the contrary, it is carefully reproduced in *Animal Farm*.

Although *Animal Farm* is mentioned in scores of studies of Orwell,[12] no critic has thought it worth a comment that the pigs who betray the revolution, like the pig who starts it, are not just pigs but boars, that is, uncastrated male pigs kept for breeding purposes. Old Major, the "prize Middle White boar" (5) who has called a meeting to tell the other animals about his dream, is initially described in terms that establish him as patriarch of this world: "He was twelve years old and had lately grown rather stout, but he was still a majestic-looking pig, with a wise and benevolent appearance in spite of the fact that his tushes had never been cut" (5–6). In contrasting his life with those of the less fortunate animals on the farm, Major says: "I am one of the lucky ones. I am twelve years old and have had over four hundred children. Such is the natural life of a pig" (10). Orwell here repeats the pattern we have seen in his other fiction, of stressing paternity as if the actual labor of reproduction were done by males. Authority comes from the phallus and fatherhood, and the sows, in fact, are hardly mentioned in the book; when they are, as we shall see, it is solely to illustrate the patriarchal control of the ruling pig, Napoleon. Leaders, then, may be good (Major) or bad (Napoleon)—but they must be male and "potent."

Contrasting with the paternal principle embodied in Major is the maternal, embodied in Clover, "a stout motherly mare approaching middle life, who had never quite got her figure back after her fourth foal" (6). Clover is characterized above all by her nurturing concern for the other animals. When a brood of ducklings that had lost their mother come into the barn, Clover "made a sort of wall round them with her great foreleg," and they nestled down inside it (7). Though Clover works along with Boxer—the enormous cart horse "as strong as any two ordinary horses put together" (6) whom Orwell uses to represent the working class, unintelligent but ever-faithful, to judge by this image—she is admired not for her hard labor but rather for her caring role as protector of the weaker animals.[13] Orwell here attributes to the maternal female dominion over the moral sphere but without any power to implement her values. As in *Nineteen Eighty-Four*, this "feminine" characteristic, though admirable, is shown to be utterly helpless and of no avail. In addition, this conventional (human) division of reality restricts the female animal to the affective and expressive sphere and the male to the instrumental.

. . . Orwell at times utilizes the same imagery in opposing ways; imagery relating to passivity, for example, is presented as attractive in "Inside the Whale" and repulsive when associated with pansy pacifists. This ambivalence is demonstrated as well in Orwell's use of protective maternal imagery. Clover's protective gesture toward the ducklings, viewed positively in *Animal Farm*, is matched by Orwell ridicule of a similar image in his verse polemic with Alex Comfort in 1943, about half a year before Orwell began composing *Animal Farm*. Falling into his familiar tough-guy rhetoric, Orwell angrily defended Churchill against pacifist gibes:

> But you don't hoot at Stalin—that's "not done"—
> Only at Churchill; I've no wish to praise him,
> I'd gladly shoot him when the war is won,
> Or now, if there were someone to replace him.
> But unlike some, I'll pay him what I owe him;
> There was a time when empires crashed like houses,
> And many a pink who'd titter at your poem
> Was glad enough to cling to Churchill's trousers.
> Christ! how they huddled up to one another
> Like day-old chicks about their foster-mother!
>   [CEJL, 2:301]

The protective environment must (as in *Coming Up for Air*) be rejected if manly status is to be preserved. But the protective gesture itself, in its inevitable futility, is admired in *Animal Farm*,[14] and it is through Clover that Orwell expresses the sadness of the failed revolution after the "purges" occur, as the stunned animals huddle around her:

> As Clover looked down the hillside her eyes filled with tears. If she could have spoken her thoughts, it would have been to say that this was not what they had aimed at when they had set themselves years ago to work for the overthrow of the human race. These scenes of terror and slaughter were not what they had looked forward to on that night when old Major first stirred them to rebellion. If she herself had had any picture of the future, it had been of a society of animals set free from hunger and the whip, all equal, each working according to his capacity, the strong protecting the weak, as she had protected the last brood of ducklings with her foreleg on the night of Major's speech. [75–76]

Clover is here contrasted with Boxer, who is unable to reflect on these matters and simply resolves to work even harder than before (74). Though Clover too "would remain faithful, work hard, carry out the orders that were given to her, and accept the leadership of Napoleon" (76), she has the moral awareness to know that "it was not for this that she and all the other animals had hoped and toiled" (76). But she lacks the words to express this awareness and instead sings "Beasts of England."

Clover stands at one of the poles of Orwell's conventional representation of female character.[15] The other pole is represented by Mollie, "the foolish, pretty white mare who drew Mr Jones's trap" (7) and is shown, early in the book, to have a link with human females. When the animals wander through the farmhouse, Mollie lingers in the best bedroom: "She had taken a piece of blue ribbon from Mrs Jones's dressing-table, and was holding it against her shoulder and admiring herself in the glass in a very foolish manner" (1–22). A less important female character is the cat who, during Major's speech, finds the warmest place to settle down in and does not listen to a word he says (7). Both Mollie and the cat, we later learn, avoid work; and Mollie is the first defector from the farm after the revolution, seduced by a neighboring farmer's offerings of ribbons for her white mane and sugar.[16]

Orwell's characterizations of old Major, Boxer, Clover, Mollie, and the cat all appear, clearly packaged and labeled, in the book's first three pages. The animal community thus forms a recognizable social world, divided by gender. This world is presented to us complete with stereotypes of patriarchal power, in the form of male wisdom, virility, or sheer strength, and female subordination, in the form of a conventional dichotomy between "good" maternal females and "bad" nonmaternal females. It is difficult to gauge Orwell's intentions in making use of gender stereotypes in *Animal Farm*. Given the evidence of his other texts, however, it seems unlikely that the possibility of a critical, even satirical, account of gender divisions ever crossed his mind. Perhaps he simply incorporated the familiar into his animal fable as part of the "natural human" traits needed to gain plausibility for his drama of a revolution betrayed. But in so doing he inadvertently reveals something very important about this barnyard revolution: Like its human counterparts, it invariably recreates the institution of patriarchy.

Sexual Politics on the Farm

Not only does Orwell's satire of a Marxist ("Animalist") revolution fail to question gender domination while arguing against species domination, it actually depends upon the stability of patriarchy as an institution. This is demonstrated by the continuity between Mr. Jones, the original proprietor of the farm, and Napoleon (Stalin), the young boar who contrives to drive out Snowball (Trotsky), the only competing boar on the premises, and assumes Jones's former position as well as that of Major, the old patriarch.

In her study of feminism and socialism, Batya Weinbaum attempts to explain why socialist revolutions have tended to reestablish patriarchy. Describing this pattern in the Russian and Chinese revolutions, Weinbaum utilizes the terminology of kin categories: father, daughter, brother, wife. These categories allow her to point out that revolutions have expressed the revolt of brothers against fathers. Though her analysis relies on a Freudian model of sexual rivalry, agreement about motivation is not necessary in order to see the value of the kin categories she proposes. While daughters participate along with brothers in the early stages of revolution, they are increasingly left out of the centers of power once the brothers realize they can occupy the positions formerly held by the fathers, thus gaining privileged access to the labor and services of women.[17]

It is intriguing to note how closely this scheme fits *Animal Farm*. Although Orwell describes a generalized revolt of the animals, inspired by a wise father's message of freedom, this revolt against the human exploiter Jones is quickly perverted into a struggle between two of the brothers, each eager to occupy the father slot and eliminate his competitor. Orwell makes it explicit that the struggle goes on between the only two boars among the pigs. The male porkers (castrated pigs) are not contenders for the father role. There is even an especially nasty portrayal of Squealer, the public relations porker who, in keeping with Orwell's other slurs against the press, is depicted as devoid of masculinity (in Orwell's terms): He stays safely away from the fighting. Once Napoleon wins out over Snowball, we see just what the father role means in terms of access to females. As the sole potent male pig on the farm, Napoleon is of course the father of the next generation of elite pigs: "In the autumn the four sows had all littered about simultaneously, producing thirty-one young pigs between them. The young pigs were piebald, and as Napoleon was the only boar on the farm, it was possible to guess at their parentage" (96).

In addition, the relations among the sows, competing for Napoleon's favor, are hinted at near the story's end, when Napoleon is on the verge of complete reconciliation with the human fathers, the neighboring farmers. Orwell informs us that the pigs (males) began to wear Mr. Jones's clothes, "Napoleon himself appearing in a black coat, ratcatcher breeches, and leather leggings, while his favourite sow appeared in the watered silk dress which Mrs. Jones had been used to wearing on Sundays" (115). Perhaps because these details seem to be beside the point in terms of the allegory, they are all the more intriguing as instances of Orwell's fantasy at work. Intentionally or not, Orwell has re-created the structure of the patriarchal family. As in human families, power among the pigs is organized along two axes: sex and age.

Though we are told that the pigs as a whole exploit the other animals (by keeping more and better food for themselves, claiming exemption from physical labor because they are doing the "brainwork" of the farm, and finally moving into the farmhouse and adopting all the formerly proscribed human habits), it is only the male pigs whom we see, in the book's closing line, as indistinguishable from human males: "The creatures outside looked from pig to man, and from man to pig, and from pig to man again; but already it was impossible to say which was which" (120). Piggish adaptation to the human world involves not only the general class discrimination evident in the rewritten Commandment: "All animals are equal but some animals are more equal than others"(114).[18] It also appears more specifically in the gender hierarchy that culminates in this last scene, so different from the account of the revolution itself in which virtually all the animals and both sexes had participated. Even as the animal allegory duplicates Orwell's gender assumptions, it also liberates him to some extent from the confines of his own androcentric framework. This is apparent in the unfolding of old Major's speech early in the book. He begins with general comments about the animals' lot: "No animal in England knows the meaning of happiness or leisure after he is a year old. No animal in England is free. The life of an animal is misery and slavery: that is the plain truth" (8). But as he continues to speak, his emphasis shifts slightly:

> Why then do we continue in this miserable condition? Because nearly the whole of our produce is stolen from us by human beings. There, comrades, is the answer to all our problems. It is summed up in a single word—Man. Man is the only real enemy we have. Remove Man from the scene, and the root cause of hunger and overwork is abolished forever.
>
> Man is the only creature that consumes without producing. He does not give milk, he does not lay eggs, he is too weak to pull the plough, he cannot run fast enough to catch rabbits. [8–9]

Here, for the first and only time in his writings, Orwell recognizes female reproductive labor as part and parcel of a society's productive activities and as a form of labor that gives females the right to make political and economic demands. In old Major's speech, it is this female labor, specifically, that becomes the most dramatic focal point. The passage quoted above continues:

> Yet he [Man] is lord of all the animals. He sets them to work, he gives back to them the bare minimum that will prevent them

from starving, and the rest he keeps for himself. Our labour tills the soil, our dung fertilizes it, and yet there is not one of us that owns more than his bare skin. You cows that I see before me, how many thousands of gallons of milk have you given during this last year? And what has happened to that milk which should have been breeding up sturdy calves? Every drop of it has gone down the throats of our enemies. And you hens, how many eggs have you laid this year, and how many of those eggs ever hatched into chickens? The rest have all gone to market to bring in money for Jones and his men. And you, Clover, where are those four foals you bore, who should have been the support and pleasure of your old age? Each was sold at a year old—you will never see one of them again. In return for your four confinements and all your labour in the field, what have you ever had except your bare rations and a stall? [9]

In this passage Orwell is finally able to make the connection between "public" and "private"—between the male's (typical) work of production and the female's (typical) work of reproduction. He sees that both forms of labor can be expropriated and that the "private" sphere in which relations of caring and nurturing go on is very much a part of the overall system of exploitation that old Major protests. Thinking about animals, Orwell notices that females are insufficiently rewarded for the labor stolen from them by men.

As the revolution decays, there occurs an episode in which Napoleon forces the hens to give up more of their eggs, so that they can be used for export to a neighboring farm. At first the hens sabotage this plan by dropping their eggs from the rafters of the barn. But they are quickly brought into line by the cessation of their rations (the acquisition of food still not being under their direct control). After holding out for five days, the hens capitulate (66–67). This increased expropriation of the hens' products is viewed by Orwell in precisely the same terms as the increased labor time extracted from the other animals. In contrast, when Orwell wrote about the human working class, he never noticed the economics of reproduction or objected to women's exclusion from direct access to decent livelihoods—an exclusion justified by reference to their status as females and supposed dependents of males. It is as if, since his farm animals are not divided into individual family groupings, Orwell was able to break through the ideology of "typical family" that had earlier blinded him to the reality of women's work and position in capitalist society.

In *Animal Farm*, furthermore, Orwell touches on the problem of political expropriation of female reproductive capacity. Napoleon provides himself with a secret police force by separating a litter of newborn puppies from their mothers and rearing them himself, and these puppies, when grown up, drive out the rival brother, Snowball, and inaugurate Napoleon's reign of terror. Orwell here seems to protest against the breakup of the "natural" pattern by which the pups are suckled and raised by their mothers. This theme is reiterated when Napoleon seizes the thirty-one young pigs—his offspring—and appoints himself their instructor, so as to prepare the continued domination of pigs over the other animals in the future. Such "unnatural" expropriations stand in sharp opposition to the traditional patterns of family life so strongly supported by Orwell. The same sort of "state" interference in family life occurs, in more detailed form, in *Nineteen Eighty-Four*.

Although his fiction suggests a strong distaste for these examples of state expropriation of female reproductive labor, Orwell was actually urging the adoption in England of population policies that, if put into practice, would have openly treated women as mere vehicles for fulfilling state priorities. In "The English People," written in 1944 (that is, shortly after *Animal Farm*) though not published until 1947, Orwell, in the throes of a panic about the dwindling birthrate, exhorts the English to have more children as one of the necessary steps in order to "retain their vitality" (CEJL, 3:31). Interpreting the declining birthrate primarily as an economic problem, he urges the government to take appropriate measures:

> Any government, by a few strokes of the pen, could make childlessness as unbearable an economic burden as a big family is now: but no government has chosen to do so, because of the ignorant idea that a bigger population means more unemployed. Far more drastically than anyone has proposed hitherto, taxation will have to be graded so as to encourage child-bearing and to save women with young children from being obliged to work outside the home. [3:32]

In addition to economic and social incentives, Orwell says, a "change of outlook" is needed: "In the England of the last thirty years it has seemed all too natural that blocks of flats should refuse tenants with children, that parks and squares should be railed off to keep the children out of them, that abortion, theoretically illegal, should be looked on as a peccadillo, and that the main aim of commercial advertising should be to popularise the idea of 'having a good time' and staying young as long as possible" (3:32).

In brief, what the English must do is, among other things, to "breed faster, work harder, and probably live more simply" (3:37), a program ominously reminiscent of Napoleon's exhortation to the other animals: "The truest happiness, he said, lay in working hard and living frugally" (*Animal Farm*,

109). In Orwell's concern with socially adequate human breeding there is no more consideration for the choices of women than Napoleon shows for the desires of the hens or bitches whose eggs and puppies he removes. Orwell seems to assume that the "natural" desires of women will precisely coincide with the lines he sets out—if, that is, he has paused to look at the matter from their point of view at all. Several years later, Orwell still viewed the "population problem" in the same terms. In a newspaper column in 1947, he voices alarm that, if England does not quickly reach an average family size of four children (instead of the then existing average of two), "there will not be enough women of child-bearing age to restore the situation." He worries about where future workers will come from and again recommends financial incentives.[19] Though Orwell was hardly alone in expressing such concerns at that time, it is instructive to note the limited perspective he brings to the problem. And yet in *Nineteen Eighty-Four* he satirizes the Party's control over Outer Party members' reproductive behavior through the character of Winston's wife, Katharine, who chills Winston's blood with her commitment to regular sexual intercourse as an expression of "our duty to the Party." It seems obvious that Orwell's opinion of such state interference in sex and procreation has nothing to do with any sympathy for women as individuals but depends entirely upon his judgment of the merits of the state that is being served.

Nothing in Orwell's earlier writings reveals an awareness of the economic contributions made by women as reproducers, rearers, and caretakers of the labor force, not to mention as ordinary members of the work force. It is therefore all the more surprising that in letting his imagination translate human conflicts into animal terms this aspect of female roles at once sprang to his attention. At the same time, his female animals are still rudimentary in comparison with the more subtly drawn portraits of the male animals on the farm. The hens and cows, for example, appear primarily as good followers, prefiguring Orwell's description of Outer Party female supporters in *Nineteen Eighty-Four*. With the exception of the maternal Clover and, to a lesser extent, Mollie, the female animals are unimportant as individual actors in the fable.

The animals are differentiated not only according to gender but also by intelligence, the pigs being described as both intelligent and piggish even at an early stage in the revolution, when they appropriate the cows' milk for their own use. The other animals, with only a few exceptions, are generous, hard-working, and stupid by contrast. It is not power that corrupts the pigs; power simply provides them with the means to realize their "nature." The betrayal of the revolution in *Animal Farm*, though it occurs over a period of time, is not, in fact, described as a process. This is why *Animal Farm*, beyond what it has to say concerning Stalin and the Soviet Union, has a profoundly dispiriting message. Orwell presents a static picture of a static universe in which the notion of the pigs' animal nature explains what happens. The final tableau, with the pigs and the men indistinguishable, is the actualization of the potential inherent in the pigs from the beginning. Unlike what he does in *Nineteen Eighty-Four*, however, Orwell gives the pigs specific material motives for the exploitation of the other animals: better food, more leisure, and a privileged life, all acquired partly by terrorizing and partly by gulling the others into thinking that because the pigs are more intelligent they alone can manage the farm. The question of intelligence is a problematic one in this book, for Orwell associates this characteristic with exploitation. There is a suggestion here that generosity, cooperation, devotion are somehow incompatible with intelligence. The deeper question, of what power hunger is really about, is avoided, and the apparent answers Orwell provides in his animal fable are inconsistent and unsatisfying, for even among the pigs not all are shown to be corrupted by greed and the desire for power.

As the pigs duplicate the human model of social organization, they not only reproduce the pattern of patriarchy already familiar to the animals (judging by Major's status early in the book!) but add to it those human characteristics that Orwell found most reprehensible—especially softness. They slowly adopt Mr. Jones's manner of living, complete with cushy bed and booze. This is contrasted with the heroic labor of the immensely strong Boxer, who literally works himself to death. Relations between the pigs and the other animals follow the patriarchal model also in that they are hierarchical and discipline-oriented; submission and obedience are extracted from the worker animals as the price of the supposedly indispensable pig leadership.

In addition to the touching solidarity evident among the worker animals, some individual relationships also emerge. One of these is the nonverbal "masculine" friendship between Boxer and Benjamin, who look forward to their retirement together. There is no female version of this friendship, however. Instead, Clover plays the role not only of maternal mare to the other animals but also of "wife"—to use Weinbaum's kin categories again—in that she has a heart-to-heart talk with Mollie. Cast in the role of the rebellious "daughter" who refuses to adhere to the farm's values, Mollie disbelieves in the communal cause and prefers to ally herself with powerful human males outside the farm, thus assuring her easier life as a kept and well-decorated mare. Orwell signals his disapproval of Mollie by showing her cowardice (39) as well as her vanity and sloth. Given the revolution's eventual outcome, however, Mollie's behavior, though egocentric, is not as misguided as it may seem. Orwell makes it explicit that under the rule of Napoleon the animals (except the pigs and Moses, the raven, who represents the church) have an even more arduous work life than animals on the neighboring (i.e., capitalist) farms.

Mollie might better be viewed as having some spontaneous understanding of the rules of patriarchy, characterized by Weinbaum in these words: "Brothers may step across the line to become fathers; but daughters face a future as a powerless wife."[20]

Animal Farm As a Feminist Fable

With astonishing ease and aptness, *Animal Farm* can be read as a feminist critique of socialist revolutions which, through their failure to challenge patriarchy, have reproduced patriarchal values in the postrevolutionary period. In this reading of the fable, the pigs would be the sole male animals, while most of the other animals are stereotyped females: compliant, hardworking drones brainwashed with the illusion that their work is done for themselves, surrendering the fruits of their productive and reproductive labor to their masters, who tell them that there never was hope of a different future.

As in the power relations between men and women, so in *Animal Farm* "science" is used to explain that pigs need better and bigger rations because they are "brain workers," an argument offering the additional message that the dependent animals could not manage on their own. These brainworkers take on the "hard" work of supervising the political and economic life of the farm, consigning the rest to the "less important" tasks of physical labor and maintenance of the farm/home. By also assuming the burden of "international" relations (with neighboring farms), the pigs keep the others pure from any contaminating contact with the outside world—again, an uncanny parallel to the public/private split of ordinary patriarchal society. Whether the individual nonpig animal is big and strong like Boxer or small and weak like the hens, it is held in check by an ideology of its own ignorance and dependence, subjected to violence and intimidation, and urged to sacrifice itself. Such an animal is not likely to rebel. But, as Orwell himself pointed out, the book does not end on a totally pessimistic note. For in the recognition that pigs and men are identical lies the spark of knowledge that can lead to liberatory action.

It would be absurd, of course, to suggest that Orwell intended such a feminist reading of his text. Everything he ever wrote shows that he took the patriarchal family to be the proper model of society. In "The Lion and the Unicorn" he complained only that England was like "a family with the wrong members in control,"

> a rather stuffy Victorian family, with not many black sheep in it but with all its cupboards bursting with skeletons. It has rich relations who have to be kow-towed to and poor relations who are horribly sat upon, and there is a deep conspiracy of silence about the source of the family income. It is a family in which the young are generally

thwarted and most of the power is in the hands of irresponsible uncles and bedridden aunts. Still, it is a family. It has its private language and its common memories, and at the approach of an enemy it closes its ranks. [CEJL, 2:68]

Of course, Orwell's version of just who is in control itself indicates his habitual misreading of the status of women in his own society. It seems to me that Orwell's complaint was on behalf of the brothers alone, as evidenced by his lack of awareness of the real disunity inherent in the patriarchal family.[21]

It is fascinating to see Orwell describe the betrayal of the animals' revolution in terms so suggestive of women's experience under patriarchy. It is women who, more than any other group and regardless of the race and class to which they belong, have had their history obliterated, their words suppressed and forgotten, their position in society confounded by the doublethink of "All men are created equal," their legal rights denied, their labor in the home and outside of it expropriated and controlled by men, their reproductive capacities used against them, their desire for knowledge thwarted, their strivings turned into dependence—all of these under the single pretext that they are not "by nature" equipped to do the valued work of society, defined as what men do. When read as a feminist fable, however, *Animal Farm* has another important message. The origins of the Seven Commandments of Animalism lie in Major's warnings against adopting Man's ways: "And remember also that in fighting against Man, we must not come to resemble him. Even when you have conquered him, do not adopt his vices" (11–12).

Orwell knew that something was missing from his political analysis, however, as is apparent in one of his "As I Please" columns dating from November 1946, in which he examines the front page of a daily newspaper and deplores the typical disasters it records. Long recovered from the quietist mood of "Inside the Whale" but now deeply pessimistic, he writes: "I think one must continue the political struggle, just as a doctor must try to save the life of a patient who is probably going to die. But I do suggest that we shall get nowhere unless we start by recognising that political behaviour is largely non-rational, that the world is suffering from some kind of mental disease which must be diagnosed before it can be cured" (CEJL, 4:248–49). . . . Orwell's next novel, *Nineteen Eighty-Four*, can help us to understand the nature of this illness.

Notes

1. Gay Clifford, *The Transformation of Allegory* (London: Routledge and Kegan Paul, 1974), pp. 7–8.
2. Ibid., p. 45.

3. Ibid., p. 36.

4. Frye's *Anatomy of Criticism* is cited by Clifford, ibid., p. 47.

5. Ibid.

6. In 1982 and 1983 I conducted an informal survey of young Americans' exposure to Orwell. About five hundred questionnaires were distributed to undergraduates in state universities on the East Coast, the West Coast, and in the Midwest. Although nearly half the students said they had read either *Animal Farm* or *Nineteen Eighty-Four* (occasionally both), usually in junior high school or high school, few could remember anything about the books. Most could not comment on Orwell's politics, but those who did so almost unanimously identified him as an anti-Communist, or, as one student wrote: "I would say that Orwell is anti-communist (socialist)." Others wrote: "He was concerned with the rise in socialism and the control it was coming to have"; "Believed nothing should take away from strength of private sector, that is, the individual. Despised totalitarianism but was not totally satisfied with complete democracy either"; "Society is heading toward a state of socialism and totalitarian rule"; "He likes animals." Rarely did a student know that Orwell considered himself a socialist. Several students had read *The Road to Wigan Pier* in an English history course at one university. Of these, one said Orwell was "anti-industrialist," and another said "he was a socialist." One student had read *Animal Farm* in a course on satire the year before and commented that in this work Orwell "acknowledged the fact that men are not of equal intelligence and, therefore, will not be able to achieve a pure social and political equality. He saw corruption as an inherent trait of any governing body." A student who remembered *Animal Farm* from junior high school wrote: "There will always be a ruling class—the lower class, upon taking over the upper class, will in turn become the ruling, upper class."

The Berg Collection, New York Public Library, holds several letters from Orwell to Leonard Moore in July 1949 in which Orwell expresses his willingness to subsidize a translation of *Animal Farm* made by some Russian Displaced Persons in Germany who wanted to smuggle the translation through the Iron Curtain.

7. Thomas N. Carter, "Group Psychological Phenomena of a Political System as Satirized in 'Animal Farm': An Application of the Theories of W. R. Bion," *Human Relations* 27, no. 2 (June 1974): 525.

8. Ellen Douglass Leyburn, *Satiric Allegory: The Mirror of Man* (New Haven: Yale University Press, 1956), p. 60.

9. Katharine Burdekin [Murray Constantine], *Proud Man* [London: Boriswood, 1934], p. 17.

10. For an insightful discussion of the role of womb envy in the maintenance of misogyny and patriarchy, see Eva Feder Kittay, "Womb Envy: An Explanatory Concept," in Joyce Trebilcot, ed., *Mothering: Essays in Feminist Theory* (Totowa, N.J.: Rowman and Allanheld, 1984), pp. 94–128. In this, as in other respects, Katharine Burdekin was ahead of her time. For further discussion of the relevance of Burdekin's work to Orwell's.

11. *Letter to Leonard Moore*, December 17, 1947, Berg Collection, New York Public Library. Quoted in Alex Zwerdling, *Orwell and the Left* (New Haven and London: Yale University Press, 1974), p. 90.

12. For a book almost universally acclaimed, *Animal Farm* has been subjected to very little serious analysis. Writing in 1950, Tom Hopkinson declared it to be one of two contemporary books before which the critic had to abdicate (cited in John Atkins, *George Orwell* [New York: Frederick Ungar, 1954], p. 221). This perspective was

adopted by many critics, perhaps as justification for their lack of response (beyond the obvious political one) to the work. Thus, for example, Atkins himself declared, "There is only one thing to do with *Animal Farm* at this stage, apart from reading it" (p. 222), and proceeded to give, yet again, the political parallels between Orwell's text and Soviet history in the period between 1917 and 1943. George Woodcock, *The Crystal Spirit: A Study of George Orwell* (Boston: Little, Brown, 1966), p. 193, repeats this line of commentary, stating that Orwell succeeded admirably in achieving his aim (of fusing political purpose and artistic purpose in one whole, as Orwell himself had explained in "Why I Write"), and then says that in *Animal Farm* Orwell "produced a book so clear in intent and writing that the critic is usually rather nonplussed as to what he should say about it; all is so magnificently there, and the only thing that really needs to be done is to place this crystalline little book into its proper setting." If this kind of reasoning were genuinely valid, then all literary criticism would stand as a monument to the failure of the works that inspired it! Another typical example of critical treatment of *Animal Farm* is Frank W. Wadsworth's essay "Orwell's Later Work," *University of Kansas City Review*, June 1956. Wadsworth states (p. 285) that *Animal Farm*'s "technical brilliance cannot, of course, be denied" and affirms that it is "a great deal more than mere political satire," but what precisely it is he does not then specify, preferring to turn his attention to *Nineteen Eighty-Four*. It is hard to avoid the conclusion that were *Animal Farm* a satire of capitalism, of equal "technical brilliance," it would not have achieved such fame. Since Orwell's reputation in the world-at-large (as opposed to the smaller world of literary criticism) rests largely on *Animal Farm* and his other anti-Communist work, *Nineteen Eighty-Four*, this is a relevant consideration. But, as Orwell himself stated repeatedly, it is difficult, if not impossible, to separate political from "aesthetic" responses to a work. Nor can one argue that Orwell is "not responsible" for the conservative political uses made of his work. As Louis Althusser comments, in "Cremonini, Painter of the Abstract," *Lenin and Philosophy and Other Essays* (New York and London: Monthly Review Press, 1971), p. 242, "a great artist cannot fail to take into account in his work itself, in its disposition and internal economy, the ideological *effects* necessarily produced by its existence. Whether this assumption of responsibility is completely lucid or not is a *different* question" (Althusser's emphasis). Orwell in effect acknowledges this. One of his letters (in the Berg Collection, New York Public Library) to Leonard Moore, dated January 9, 1947, comments on the serialization in a "reactionary" Dutch publication of a translation of *Animal Farm*. Orwell writes: "Obviously a book of that type is liable to be made use of by Conservatives, Catholics etc."

13. Robert A. Lee, *Orwell's Fiction* (Notre Dame, Ind.: University of Notre Dame Press, 1969), notes that Boxer's stupidity "suggests interesting qualifications about Orwell's reputed love of the common man, qualifications which become even stronger in light of the description of the proles in *1984*." Lee further comments that "Clover is more intelligent and perceptive than is Boxer, but she has a corresponding lack of strength. Her 'character' is primarily a function of her sex. Her instincts are maternal and pacifistic. She works hard, along with the other animals, but there is no picture of any special strength, as there is with Boxer. And even with a greater intelligence, her insights are partial" (p. 123). "A paradigm appears," Lee concludes: "Boxer is marked by great strength and great stupidity; Clover has less physical power but has a corresponding increase in awareness; the equation is completed with Benjamin [the donkey] who sees and knows most—perhaps all—but is physically

ineffectual and socially irresponsible" (p. 124). Lee's commentary on *Animal Farm* is far more interesting and insightful than most.

14. J. R. Osgerby, "'Animal Farm' and 'Nineteen Eighty Four,'" *The Use of English* 17, no. 3 (Spring 1966): 237–43, discusses the theme of compassion and the "protective gesture" in these two books, noting the permutations of this gesture until it culminates in a grim parody at the end of *Nineteen Eighty-Four* as Winston clings to O'Brien like a baby.

15. Orwell's description of Clover as "the motherly mare approaching middle life" recalls his preference for such maternal figures. In a column describing an ideal (imaginary) pub, "The Moon under Water," he specifies that the barmaids "are all middle-aged women" who call everyone "dear" rather than "ducky"; the latter, he says, is typical of pubs with "a disagreeable raffish atmosphere" (CEJL, 3:45).

16. As an illustration of how little the terms of such denigration have changed, consider the misogynistic satire of Semonides of Amorgos who, in the seventh century B.C., wrote a poem describing ten types of women, most of them formed by Zeus out of different animals. All except the hardworking bee are depicted in negative terms. Semonides describes the "mare-woman" thus: "Another was the offspring of a proud mare with a long mane. She pushes servile work and trouble on to others; she would never set her hand to a mill, nor pick up a sieve nor throw the dung out of the house, nor sit over the oven dodging the soot; she makes her husband acquainted with Necessity. She washes the dirt off herself twice, sometimes three times, every day; she rubs herself with scents, and always has her thick hair combed and garlanded with flowers. A woman like her is a fine sight for others, but for the man she belongs to she proves a plague, unless he is some tyrant or king [who takes pride in such objects]" (in Hugh Lloyd-Jones, "Females of the Species: On 118 Lines of Semonides," *Encounter*, May 1975, p. 53; Lloyd-Jones's brackets). I am indebted to Barbara Halporn of Indiana University for this reference.

17. Batya Weinbaum, *The Curious Courtship of Women's Liberation and Socialism* (Boston: South End Press, 1978), chap. 8. A related critique is Heidi Hartmann, "The Unhappy Marriage of Marxism and Feminism," reprinted in Lydia Sargent, ed., *Women and Revolution: A Discussion of the Unhappy Marriage of Marxism and Feminism* (Boston: South End Press, 1981).

18. Richard Mayne recently pointed out, in the *Times Literary Supplement*, November 26, 1982, that Orwell's most famous line is in fact borrowed from another writer, Philip Guedalla. Guedalla's "A Russian Fairy Tale," *The Missing Muse* (New York: Harper and Brothers, 1930), is a brief anti-Communist satire in which there appears a Good Fairy "who believed that all fairies were equal before the law, but held strongly that some fairies were more equal than others" (p. 206). Guedalla, however, throws the line away, while Orwell creates a context that makes it unforgettable. Nonetheless, it is instructive that the one line in all Orwell's prose that critics repeatedly point to as the pinnacle of Orwell's achievement in clarity and concision in fact was not composed by him. Raymond Williams, for example, in *Orwell* (Glasgow: Fontana/Collins, 1971), p. 74, cites this line as an example of the "exceptionally strong and pure prose" Orwell was "able to release" in *Animal Farm*. Orwell himself, incidentally, did not hesitate to use the word "plagiarism" in relation to far less precise borrowings, as when he commented, in a letter to Fred Warburg, that Aldous Huxley had clearly "plagiarized" to some extent from Eugene Zamiatin's *We* in composing *Brave New World* (CEJL, 4:485).

19. "As I Please," *Tribune*, March 21, 1947, p. 13; on file in the Orwell Archive. In *Crystal Spirit*, p. 284, George Woodcock notes that Orwell saw the family "as a morally regenerating institution; and birth control and abortion as manifestations of moral degeneration," but Woodcock disregards the gender ideology expressed by these attitudes.

20. Weinbaum, *Curious Courtship*, p. 96.

21. Heidi I. Hartmann, "The Family as the Locus of Gender, Class, and Political Struggle: The Example of Housework," *Signs* 6, no. 3 (Summer 1981): 372. Hartmann in this essay challenges the idea that the family is an active agent with unified interests and focuses on housework to illustrate the different material interests among family members caused by their differing relations to patriarchy and capitalism. She shows that men's work in the house does not increase proportionally to women's work outside of the house and concludes that "patriarchy appears to be a more salient feature than class" in understanding women's work in the home (p. 386). She refers to studies indicating this is also true in very different societies, e.g., Bangladesh, which confirm that men's lives are more altered by class distinctions than women's.

VALERIE MEYERS

Animal Farm: *An Allegory of Revolution*

So far is it from being true that men are naturally equal, that no two
people can be half an hour together, but one shall acquire an evident
superiority over the other.

> Samuel Johnson, quoted in James Boswell, *Life of Johnson*

In spite of Orwell's well-known opposition to continued British rule in India
(where *Burmese Days* was banned) he was hired in August 1941 to produce
programmes for the Indian section of the BBC's Eastern Service, to counter Japanese and German radio propaganda. Two million Indian volunteer
troops were fighting on the British side, and the BBC's task was to maintain
Indian support. For more than two years Orwell prepared weekly news bul-
letins, commissioned cultural talks and discussions, adapted stories, wrote
dialogues and reviews. Because paper was in short supply, newspapers and
magazines, the outlets for Orwell's work, were very restricted. Broadcasting
allowed him to keep up his political comment and literary journalism. W. J.
West has convincingly suggested that Orwell's experience in radio adaptation and in condensing, simplifying and arranging information for propaganda purposes largely accounts for the success of *Animal Farm*—its speed
of composition (Orwell completed it in three months, after leaving the BBC
in November 1943), its clarity and conciseness, its universality of appeal, its
radically different form from any of Orwell's previous work.[49]

From *George Orwell*, pp. 101–13, 149–50. © 1991 by Valerie Meyers.

'*Animal Farm*', Orwell wrote, 'was the first book in which I tried, with full consciousness of what I was doing, to fuse political purpose and artistic purpose into one whole' (*CEJL*, 1.7). In his preface to the Ukrainian edition, published in 1947, Orwell said that he wanted to write the book in a simple language because he wanted to tell ordinary English people, who had enjoyed a tradition of justice and liberty for centuries, what a totalitarian system was like. His experience in Spain had shown him 'how easily totalitarian propaganda can control the opinion of enlightened people in democratic countries' and he wrote the book to destroy the 'Soviet myth' that Russia was a truly socialist society (*CEJL*, 3.404).

In the 1930s European intellectuals idealised the Soviet Union. Even E. M. Forster, a relatively non-political writer, commented in an essay of 1934, 'no political creed except communism offers an intelligent man any hope'.[50] Throughout the 1930s Orwell had been sceptical about the Soviet version of current events in Russia; in Spain he saw Spanish Communists, directed by Moscow, betray their allies. In the late 1930s news reached the West of the infamous Purge Trials, which took the lives of three million people and sent countless others to forced labour camps in order to make Stalin's power absolute. In 1939 Stalin signed a non-aggression pact with Hitler, which allowed the Germans to overrun Poland and Czechoslovakia. Orwell's indignant reaction to these events provoked him to write this powerful pamphlet.

The Genre of *Animal Farm*

Orwell particularly valued the vigorous, colourful and concrete style of pamphlets and wanted to revive the genre. *Animal Farm* was his contribution to the English tradition of Utopian pamphlets, which originated in Thomas More's *Utopia* (1516). Like *Utopia*, *Animal Farm* is brief, light and witty, but has a serious purpose. More's pamphlet attacked the monarch's excessive power and the cruel dispossession of tenant-farmers by the lords who enclosed lands for sheep-grazing; Orwell's attacks the injustice of the Soviet regime and seeks to correct Western misconceptions about Soviet Communism.

More invented the device of satirising contemporary society by contrasting it with a traveller's account of a distant country. His narrator talks to Raphael Hythloday, who has just returned from Utopia (a name derived from the Greek, meaning 'no place' or 'nowhere'). In contrast to the majority of Englishmen, who suffer poverty and constant war, the Utopians are rational and kind, own everything in common and share everything equally. War, envy, greed and pursuit of personal riches or power are unknown.

More's narrator remarks sceptically that he 'cannot conceive of authority among men that are equal to one another in all things'.[51] He cannot imagine a world where no one has greater status or wealth than anyone else. More raised the fundamental question, which Orwell took up centuries later, of whether it is possible for men to live together fairly, justly and equally. More's answer is ethical: that there is no point in changing our social system unless we change our morality; his pamphlet urges us to take responsibility for improving our society. While More's Utopia is totally imaginary, Orwell's Animal Farm is based on the first thirty years of the Soviet Union, a real society pursuing the ideal of equality. His book argues that this kind of society hasn't worked, and couldn't.

Orwell said that Jonathan Swift's *Gulliver's Travels* (1726) 'has meant more to me than any other book ever written'.[52] Far longer and more complex than *Utopia*, it uses the same device of a traveller's tales to attack contemporary society, but the various places Gulliver visits are satiric renderings of aspects of English society. Orwell's Animal Farm, like Swift's Lilliput and Blefuscu, is a coded satiric portrait of a real society, an anti-utopia which, by castigating real evils, suggests what society ought to be like.

Orwell probably took a hint from the final part of *Gulliver's Travels*, Book IV, where Gulliver encounters a society formed by a superior species of horse, the Houyhnhnms, who are able to talk and conduct their lives rationally (in contrast to the savage Yahoos nearby, who, to his horror, turn out to be ape-like humans). This comparison between men and animals, in which animals are superior, may have suggested the form of Orwell's pamphlet. Orwell was also familiar with Wells's *Island of Dr Moreau*, a science-fiction novel about a doctor who turns animals into men. But this novel uses the natural goodness of animals as a contrast to the evil of modern scientific man. Unlike Swift and Wells, Orwell uses animals to symbolise human characters.

The Political Allegory

Orwell's critique of Soviet Communism is a beast-fable, a satiric form in which animals are used to represent human vice and folly. Chaucer's 'Nun's Priest's Tale', one of the *Canterbury Tales*, is an early example in English. On one level Chaucer's tale is a comic farmyard tale of a proud cock, Chanticleer, who falls prey to the fox and manages to escape; on another it is a witty and learned essay on the significance of dreams; on another, and more serious, level it is an allegory of the Fall of Man, in which Chanticleer represents Adam being tempted by the Devil. *Animal Farm*, a brief, concentrated satire, subtitled 'A Fairy Story', can also be read on the simple level of plot and character. It is an entertaining, witty tale of a farm whose oppressed animals, capable of speech and reason, overcome a cruel master and set up a revolutionary government. They are betrayed by the evil power-hungry pigs, especially by their leader, Napoleon, and forced to return to their former servitude. Only the leadership has changed. On another, more serious level, of course, it is a political allegory, a symbolic tale where all the events and characters represent events and characters in Russian history since 1917,[53] in which 'the interplay between surface action and inner meaning is everything'.[54] Orwell's deeper purpose is to teach a political lesson.

As he noted in his Ukrainian preface, Orwell used actual historical events to construct his story, but rearranged them to fit his plot. Manor Farm is Russia, Mr Jones the Tsar, the pigs the Bolsheviks who led the revolution. The humans represent the ruling class, the animals the workers and peasants. Old Major, the white boar who inspires the rebellion in the first chapter, stands for a combination of Marx, the chief theorist, and Lenin, the actual leader. Orwell makes Old Major a character whose motives are pure and idealistic, to emphasise the positive goals of the revolution, and makes him die before the rebellion itself. In actuality Lenin died in 1924, well after the revolution. Lenin himself set up the machinery of political terror which Stalin took over. The power struggle between Stalin and Trotsky (which Orwell satirises in chapter 5) happened after Lenin's death, not immediately after the revolution, as Orwell's account suggests.

The *Communist Manifesto* (1848) of Karl Marx and Friedrich Engels provided a theoretical basis for the revolutionary movements springing up in Europe in the latter part of the nineteenth century. Marx interpreted all history as the history of class struggle, arguing that the capitalist classes, or bourgeoisie, the owners of the means of production, are inevitably opposed to the interests of the wage-earning labourers, or proletariat, whom they exploit. This eternal conflict can only be resolved by revolution, when workers take over the means of production, share the fruits of their labours equally, and set up 'the dictatorship of the proletariat'. Marx's ideal was an international brotherhood of workers (for he believed that the interests of the working classes of all nations would unite them, causing them to cross barriers of race and culture, against the common enemy) and a future classless society. Old Major's speech in the first chapter parodies the ideas of the *Communist Manifesto*. He says: 'Only get rid of Man, and the produce of our labour would be our own.' Their goal should be the 'overthrow of the human race': in the coming struggle 'All men are enemies. All animals are comrades.' In chapter 3 'everyone worked according to his capacity', an echo of the Marxist slogan, 'From each according to his abilities, to each according to his needs.'

Each animal stands for a precise figure or representative type. The pigs, who can read and write and organise, are the Bolshevik intellectuals who came to dominate the vast Soviet bureaucracy. Napoleon is Stalin, the select group around him the Politburo, Snowball is Trotsky, and Squealer represents the propagandists of the regime. The pigs enjoy the privileges of belonging to the new ruling class (special food, shorter working hours), but also suffer the consequences of questioning Napoleon's policies.

The other animals represent various types of common people. Boxer the carthorse (whose name suggests the Boxer Rebellion of 1900, when revolutionaries tried to expel foreigners from China), is the decent working man, fired by enthusiasm for the egalitarian ideal, working overtime in the factories or on the land, willing to die to defend his country; Clover is the eternal, motherly working woman of the people. Molly, the unreliable, frivolous mare, represents the White Russians who opposed the revolution and fled the country; the dogs are the vast army of secret police who maintain Stalin in power; the sheep are the ignorant public who repeat the latest propaganda without thinking and who can be made to turn up to 'spontaneous demonstrations' in support of Napoleon's plans. Moses, the raven, represents the opportunist Church. He flies off after Mr Jones, but returns later, and continues to preach about the Sugarcandy Mountain (or heaven), but the pigs' propaganda obliterates any lingering belief. Benjamin the donkey, the cynical but powerless average man, never believes in the glorious future to come, and is always alert to every betrayal.

Orwell's allegory is comic in its detailed parallels: the hoof and horn is clearly the hammer and sickle, the Communist party emblem; 'Beasts of England' is a parody of the 'Internationale', the party song; the Order of the Green Banner is the Order of Lenin, and the other first- and second-class awards spoof the fondness of Soviet Russia for awarding medals, for everything from exceeding one's quota on the assembly line or in the harvest to bearing a great many children. The poem in praise of Napoleon imitates the sycophantic verses and the mass of paintings and sculptures turned out to glorify Stalin. In chapter 8, Squealer's presentation of impressive figures to show that food production had gone up, and the thin layer of grain sprinkled over the sacks to deceive Whymper, the agent, correspond to the well-known practice in totalitarian regimes of falsifying figures to project a positive image abroad.

Each event of the story has a historical parallel. The Rebellion in chapter 2 is the October 1917 Revolution, the Battle of the Cowshed in chapter 4 the subsequent Civil War. Mr Jones and the farmers represent the loyalist Russians and foreign forces who tried, but failed, to dislodge the Bolsheviks. The hens' revolt in chapter 7 stands for the brutally suppressed 1921 mutiny of the sailors at Kronstadt, which challenged the new regime to release political prisoners and grant freedoms of speech and the press. Napoleon's deal with Whymper, who trades the farm's produce at Willingdon market, represents Russia's 1922 Treaty of Rapallo with Germany. Orwell emphasises Napoleon's decision to trade because it breaks the First Commandment, that 'whatever goes upon two legs is an enemy'. Official Soviet policy was hostile to Germany, a militaristic, capitalist nation, but the Treaty revealed that the Communist regime had been trading arms and heavy machinery, and would continue to do so.

Mr Frederick of 'Pinchfield', renowned for his cruelty to animals and for appropriating others' land, represents Hitler, though his name also suggests the despotic eighteenth-century Prussian king Frederick the Great. Mr Pilkington of 'Foxwood' stands for Churchill and England, a country dominated by the fox-hunting upper classes. The Windmill stands for the first Five-Year Plan of 1928, which called for rapid industrialisation and collectivisation of agriculture. Its destruction in a storm in chapter 6 symbolises the grim failure of this policy. Chapter 7 describes in symbolic terms the famine and starvation which followed. The hens' revolt stands for the peasants' bitter resistance to collective farming, when they burned their crops and slaughtered their animals. The animals' false confessions in chapter 7 are the Purge Trials of the late 1930s. The false banknotes given by Frederick for the corn represent Hitler's betrayal of the Nazi–Soviet Pact of 1939, and the second destruction of the Windmill, by Frederick's men, is the Nazi invasion of Russia in 1941. The last chapter brings Orwell up to the date of the book's composition. He ends with a satiric portrait of the Teheran Conference of 1943, the meeting of Churchill, Roosevelt and Stalin, who are now allies. The quarrel over cheating at cards predicts the falling-out of the superpowers as soon as the war ended.

Animal Farm's apparent simplicity disguises Orwell's ingenuity in fitting all these complex historical events into a simple and persuasive plot. Like the three wishes of a fairy tale, the Seven Commandments are an effective structural device. Their stage-by-stage alteration charts the pigs' progressive rise to power and lends the narrative a tragic inevitability. This change also symbolises a key theme of the book: the totalitarian falsification of history. The pigs' gradual acquisition of privileges—apples, milk, house, whisky, beer, clothes—leads to the final identification of pig and human, Communist and capitalist.

The plot's circular movement, which returns the animals to conditions very like those in the beginning, provides occasions for vivid irony. In the first chapter they lament their forced labour and poor food, but by chapter 6 they are starving, and are forced to work once more. In chapter 1 Old Major predicts that one day Jones will send Boxer to the knacker, and in chapter 9 Napoleon fulfils the prophecy by sending him to the slaughterhouse. In chapter 7, when various animals falsely confess their crimes and are summarily executed by the dogs, 'the air was heavy with the smell of blood, which had been unknown there since the expulsion of Jones'. These ironies all emphasise the tragic failure of the revolution, and support Benjamin's view that 'life would go on as it had always gone on—that is, badly' (ch. 5).

Though all the characters are types, Orwell differentiates the two most important figures, Napoleon and Snowball, so that they resemble their real-life counterparts both in the broad lines of their characterisation and in their two major disagreements. Like Stalin, Napoleon 'has a reputation for getting his own way' (ch. 2), takes charge of indoctrinating the young, sets up an elaborate propaganda machine, cultivates an image of omnipotent, charismatic power (a 'personality cult'), surrounding himself with bodyguards and fawning attendants. Like Trotsky, Snowball is an intellectual, who quickly researches a topic and formulates plans; he is a persuasive orator, but fails to wrest the leadership from Napoleon.

Napoleon and Snowball's quarrel over the Windmill represents their dispute over what should take priority in developing the Soviet Union. Stalin wanted to collectivise agriculture, Trotsky was for developing industry. Ultimately Stalin adopted both programmes in his first Five-Year Plan, just as Napoleon derides Snowball's plans, then uses them as his own. Their most fundamental disagreement was whether to try to spread the revolution to other countries, as classical Marxism dictated, or confine themselves to making a socialist state in Russia. Napoleon argues for the latter, saying that the animals must arm themselves to protect their new leadership, Snowball that they must send more pigeons into neighbouring farms to spread the news about the revolution. Just as Stalin abandoned the idea of world revolution, so at the end Napoleon assures the farmers that he will not spread rebellion among their animals.

Expelled from the Politburo in 1925, Trotsky went into exile in 1929 and was considered a heretic. His historical role was altered, his face cut out of group photographs of the leaders of the revolution; in Russia he was denounced as a traitor and conspirator and in 1940 he was assassinated in Mexico City by a Stalinist agent. Similarly, Snowball is blamed for everything that goes wrong in Animal Farm, and the animals are persuaded that he was a traitor from the beginning. Orwell did not share the view (of Isaac Deutscher and followers of Trotsky) that the revolution would have turned out differently had Trotsky, and not Stalin, become the leader after Lenin's death. Orwell makes Snowball equally bloodthirsty and immoral. In chapter 4, as Boxer grieves over the apparent death of the stableboy whom he has kicked in the battle, Snowball urges him not to be sentimental, because 'the only good human being is a dead one'. Trotsky defended the killing of the Tsar's children, on the grounds that the murderers acted on behalf of the proletariat.[55]

It has been said that the very act of reducing human characters to animals implies a pessimistic view of man, and that in *Animal Farm* the satiric vision is close to the tragic.[56] Orwell turns elements of comedy into scenes of tragic horror. In chapter 5, for example, Napoleon comically lifts his leg to urinate on Snowball's plans. But shortly afterwards he summons the dogs and orders them to rip out the throats of those who confess their disloyalty. In one instance Napoleon's contempt is amusing, in the next horrifying. Boxer's characteristics are similarly double-edged. In chapter 3 his earnest dimwittedness contrasts amusingly with the pigs' sharpness: while he is labouring to master the alphabet, and can't get past D, Snowball is engaging in parody-dialectic, explaining that birds can be included in the rule that 'Four legs good, two legs bad', since 'A bird's wing . . . is an organ of propulsion and not of manipulation.' But Boxer's trusting simplicity also leads to his death, in one of the most moving scenes in the book.

The beast-fable is not only a device that allows Orwell's serious message to be intelligible on two levels; the use of animal to represent man is basic to his whole theme. We can readily grasp that animals are oppressed and feel it is wrong to exploit them and betray their trust. Orwell counts on our common assumptions about particular species to suggest his meaning. The sheep and their bleating are perfect metaphors for a gullible public, ever ready to accept policies and repeat rumours as truth. We commonly believe pigs are greedy and savage, even to the point of devouring their young. Orwell also uses the natural animosity of cats to sparrows, dogs to rats, to suggest the social and ethnic conflicts which belie Marx's dictum that workers' common interests outweigh differences of race and nationhood. And, most central to his theme, their 'short animal lives' suggests the book's tragic vision: that the passivity and ignorance of ordinary people allows an evil leadership to stay in power.

Orwell wanted his central figure to typify the modern dictator, whose lust for power is pathological and inhuman. Napoleon's swift, secret cruelty makes the other animals seem all too human in comparison. In a review of Hitler's *Mein Kampf*, Orwell described Napoleon, Hitler and Stalin as the quintessential modern dictators, who stayed in power for similar reasons: 'All three of the great dictators have enhanced their power by imposing intolerable burdens on their peoples' (*CEJL*, 2.14). To create Napoleon, Orwell combines aspects of both Stalin and Hitler (just as the totalitarian society in *Nineteen Eighty-Four* shares characteristics of both Stalinist Russia and Nazi Germany). The animals make enormous sacrifices to complete the Windmill, only to find that it is used to grind corn (for trade), not to make their lives easier, as Snowball had promised. Napoleon 'denounced such ideas as contrary to the spirit of Animalism. The truest happiness, he said, lay in working hard and living frugally' (ch. 10). This maxim sounds an ironic echo of the Nazi slogan 'Arbeit macht frei' ('Work liberates'), which decorated the entrance to

Auschwitz. The knacker's van which carries Boxer off to the slaughterhouse, and the deception used to induce him to enter it, recall the deportations of Jews to the death-camps, and the mobile extermination vans used to round up and murder small groups of villagers. By making Napoleon a boar Orwell also drew on the literary and historical associations of Shakespeare's *Richard III*, the literary archetype of the ugly, charismatic, absolutist schemer, whose heraldic emblem was the boar.[57]

The beast-fable form not only allowed Orwell to convey a complex message in simple terms, but was also admirably suited to his habits as a writer: his tendency to reduce characters to type, to see society as groups of competing economic interests; his narrator's detachment from the characters; his preference for grammatically simple sentences and unpretentious vocabulary. The prose succeeds brilliantly at balancing entertainment and argument because Orwell blends homely, even clichéd, language with sophisticated diction. In chapter 3, for example, 'the work of the farm went like clockwork' when the animals were in charge; into this simple fabric Orwell inserts a word with Marxist overtones: 'with the worthless *parasitical* human beings gone there was more for everyone to eat'. The context makes the word perfectly comprehensible to someone who does not know its meaning, yet if we know the word we can appreciate an additional layer of meaning—the suggestion that the animals have been indoctrinated with the Marxist view of capitalists as parasites, who own the means of production but do no work. The pleasure of reading *Animal Farm* lies in recognising the double meanings, the political and historical parallels, in the story.

In a book where distortion of language is an important theme, every word counts. Orwell's simple language points out the absurd contradictions between public political statements and private perceptions of their meaning. In chapter 6 all extra work is voluntary, but animals who refuse to do it lose half their rations; in chapter 9 Squealer announces a 'readjustment' of rations, instead of the more accurate 'reduction'. This doubletalk culminates in the last chapter, when the Commandments are reduced to one: 'All animals are equal' now has added to it 'but some are more equal than others'. The comic effect of these verbal distinctions does not diminish the tragedy of the revolution betrayed.

Orwell's Critique of Marx

Marx's most revolutionary idea is that no social form is unalterable. Since all monarchies, class systems, governments are made by man, they can be destroyed and replaced by a better, fairer system, in which men would no longer be exploited. Marx thought it historically inevitable that workers would revolt, seize the means of production, and set up a centralised government, which he termed, paradoxically, a 'dictatorship of the proletariat'. The government of the Soviet Union, however, was ruled by a new elite, a collective oligarchy, some of whom were derived from the proletariat. Orwell described such governments as 'a sham covering a new form of class-privilege' (*CEJL*, 3.320).

Orwell had always been fascinated by the corrupting effects of power and the relative weakness of good and decent people in the face of evil intelligence. In *Animal Farm* Orwell argues that, however desirable the ideal, man's instinct for power makes the classless society impossible. In his allegory, a Marxist revolution is doomed to fail, because it grants power, once again, to a select few. Major's speech 'had given to *the more intelligent animals* . . . a completely different outlook on life'.

To oppose Marx, Orwell turned to a classic seventeenth-century work of political philosophy, Thomas Hobbes's *Leviathan* (1651). A fiercely anti-revolutionary writer, Hobbes presents views of man and politics diametrically opposed to those of Marx. According to Hobbes, the life of man is 'solitary, poor, nasty, brutish and short', and all human beings are inclined to 'a perpetual and restless desire after power, which ceaseth only in death' (*Leviathan*, Book 1, ch. 11). Far from seeing men as capable of creating a new society to ensure their equality, Hobbes thought that only fear of death made men control their lust for power sufficiently to band together to form a commonwealth, an artificial machine to protect them from their enemies. For Hobbes, the one requirement of government, of whatever kind, was that it be strong enough to hold warring factions in check. He considered it inevitable that society be divided into social classes.

There are several important echoes of Hobbes in *Animal Farm*. Ironically, Marx-Major paraphrases Hobbes in the first chapter, when he says, 'our lives are miserable, laborious, and short'. In the last chapter, when the animals can no longer remember the promises of the revolution, Benjamin expresses the Hobbesian opinion that 'hunger, hardship and disappointment . . . [are] the unalterable law of life'. Alone of all the animals, Benjamin refuses either to hope or be disappointed, and his commentary often suggests a Swiftian cynicism, such as when he refuses to read, on the ground that there is nothing worth reading. This choice turns out to be the wise one, when we consider how the written word has been manipulated by the pigs.

But we should not assume that Benjamin's voice represents Orwell's. Orwell did not agree with Hobbes's political philosophy, nor did he, like Swift, find mankind ultimately disgusting. He simply believed that the rise of Russian totalitarianism could best be explained by Hobbes's theory, rather than by Marx's. Orwell summed up his attitude to revolution in the preface to a collection of British pamphlets:

The most encouraging fact about revolutionary activity is that, although it always fails, it always continues. The vision of a world of free and equal human beings, living together in a state of brotherhood—in one age it is called the Kingdom of Heaven, in another the classless society—never materialises, but the belief in it never seems to die out.[58]

Orwell had great difficulty publishing *Animal Farm*, which he completed in February 1943, for Russia had become an ally in the war against Germany, and was suffering heavy losses. Though he praised the style and compared it to Swift, T. S. Eliot, a director of Faber, spoke for most publishers when he rejected it because 'we have no conviction that this is the right point of view from which to criticise the political situation at the present time'. He told Orwell that he found the ending unsatisfactory because 'your pigs are far more intellectual than the other animals, and therefore the best qualified to run the farm', and that clearly all that was needed was 'more public-spirited pigs',[59] though, as Orwell's book shows, revolutionary leaders are rarely public-spirited. Finally published in August 1945, *Animal Farm* was given the highest praise by Graham Greene and by Edmund Wilson, but some critics refused to accept the validity of Orwell's attack on Soviet Communism. Cyril Connolly defended Russia, asserting that 'despite a police system which we should find intolerable, the masses are happy, and . . . great strides in material progress have been made'.[60] Northrop Frye considered the allegory superficial, and sneered at the ending, asserting that the moral of the book is 'the reactionary bromide' that 'you can't change human nature'.[61] But Orwell's book does not pretend to be a probing analysis of Russian Communism. His purpose was to expose the totalitarian nature of the Russian government in as simple and effective a form as possible, and in this he succeeded. It is a cautionary tale, but what it suggests about power and revolution is not reducible to a formula.

As for the criticism that Orwell's satire is exaggerated, the book's continued popularity (in illegal editions) in Eastern Europe shows that his satire is as accurate as it is enduring. As recently as September 1987, customs officials at the Moscow International Book Fair cleared the British exhibitors' shelves of *Animal Farm*. There can be no better certification of its truth.

Notes

49. *Orwell: The Lost Writings*, ed. W. J. West (New York: Arbor House, 1985), p. 61. (Published in Great Britain as *Orwell: The War Broadcasts*.)

50. E. M. Forster, 'A Note on the Way' (1934), in *Abinger Harvest* (New York: Meridian, 1955), p. 72.

51. Thomas More, *Utopia* (New York: Appleton-Century-Crofts, 1949), p. 26.

52. *Orwell: The Lost Writings*, p. 112.

53. See Jeffrey Meyers, *A Reader's Guide to George Orwell*, pp. 130–143.

54. Woodcock, *The Crystal Spirit*, p. ix.

55. See Paul Johnson, *Modern Times* (New York: Harper and Row, 1985), p. 263.

56. Stephen Greenblatt, 'Orwell as Satirist', in *George Orwell: A Collection of Critical Essays*, p. 108.

57. See *Richard III*, II.ii.28. Richard, like Stalin, puts his unsuspecting, innocent victims to death.

58. *British Pamphleteers*, vol. 1 (London: Allan Wingate, 1948), Introduction by Orwell, p. 10.

59. In *George Orwell: The Critical Heritage*, p. 20.

60. Ibid., p. 200.

61. Ibid., p.208.

SAMIR ELBARBARY

Language as Theme in Animal Farm

George Orwell's repeated insistence on plain, firm language reflects his confidence in ordinary truth. This is visible in the language of the narrator in *Animal Farm*, which is characterized by syntactic tidiness and verbal pithiness. "Mr. Jones, of the Manor Farm, had locked the hen-houses for the night, but was too drunk to remember to shut the pop-holes"; this is how the narrator begins the fable. Set in ironic juxtaposition to this terse phrasing is another distinct language: the crassly elitist, manipulative, unintelligible, and circumlocutory discourse of the pigs, through which the fictitious passes off as factitious and the animals' world is created for them. The magical agency in this fairy tale takes the form of language which becomes a distorting mirror rather than a clear pane.[1] I suggest that the deliberate derangement of language, and linguistic exclusiveness which sustain the usurpation of power, stand out as one of the novel's central thematic concerns. In a sense, the revolution on the farm is a language-focused enterprise, a product of specifically aggressive linguistic energy, and language, which can effectively control reality, is at the root of the tragic experience rather than merely mirroring it. The animals are the negative other of the pigs. They—with an underdeveloped language, a para-language—are overpowered by the linguistic skill of the pigs; their ensnarement is less a matter of substance than of generic linguistic

From *The International Fiction Review* 19, no. 1 (1992): 31–38. © 1992 by International Fiction Association.

impotence and deficient semantic memory. They are incompetent readers of the pigs' devious texts.

The beginning of the narrative quickly establishes the primacy of language. The character of old Major, who dominates the scene of this section, is reduced to a mouth. In a lengthy address to the animals, he engages in a verbal creation of what society might become. He is the "man on the white horse" who steps in with utopian discourse. A nocturnal time setting (Major "was so highly regarded on the farm that everyone was quite ready to lose an hour's sleep in order to hear what he had to say"[2]) lends to the situation a layer of fantasy. Major speaks from above ("a sort of raised platform" [1]—perhaps a symbol of the sacred locus of revelation, distance also marks separation) and offers his text in the light of the received major prophecy. Attacks are heaped upon man. With his elocutionary style and the accent of exhortation, Major creates an atmosphere of paternalism; there is a disparity between the liberating stance and authoritative language structure. Beside the hammering imperative tone ("You cows"; "And you hens"; "And you Clover"; "get rid of Man"; "work night and day"; "Fix your eyes on that"; "pass on this message" 4–5) there is his willful persistence in the use of the first person (15 "I"s in one short paragraph; 3). He sets sights idealistically high about forming a happy collectivity with a manna economy. His general prescription that getting rid of man will bring an overnight change is delivered as gospel. The dramatic speech moves incrementally to a climactic point: " . . . only get rid of Man, and the produce of our labour would be our own. Almost overnight we could become rich and free" (5). According to Major, the society of the future is marked by spontaneous fraternization: "All animals are comrades" (6). In a supreme cautionary irony, the dogs suddenly chase the rats, substituting a truth for the lie and deconstructing the preceding platitude. Yet, this is lost on the animals. Major, too, is not aware that the animals will suffer under the pigs what he predicts will come if revolution does not take place. There is a grim irony in this: "To that horror we all must come—cows, pigs, hens, sheep, everyone. Even the horses and the dogs have no better fate. You, Boxer, the very day that those great muscles of yours lose their power, Jones will sell you to the knacker, who will cut your throat and boil you down for the foxhounds" (5). The oration has cunningly generated an emotional momentum which carries the animals incarcerated along with it. Their experience as naive readers seduced by the text can be viewed in terms of pleasure. Major climaxes his linguistic construct with a patriotic hymn that finds a response in the animals' euphoria (7–8). His linguistic fantasy is virtually a deathbed utterance. "Three nights later," we read, "Major died peacefully in his sleep" (9). The high ideals are as dead as Major himself. It is of significance for Orwell's deconstruction that the visionary potential is shrouded in darkness.

A rhetorical ploy that Major uses to lease ears is varying the type of sentence structure, and varying the usual declarative statement with questions, exclamations, exhortations, and other moods of discourse. Anaphoric repetition—the repeated word "And" at the beginning of consecutive paragraphs—is another device used, creating a bouncing rhythm. This helps form cross-correspondences and build the expansion of the discourse to a climax. More still are the refrain-like restatements of the same point: "Man is the only real enemy we have, "All men are enemies," "Whatever goes upon two legs is an enemy," "remember always your duty of enmity towards Man." Ironical use of Oxymoron appears later in the novel in structures such as: "This work was strictly voluntary, but any animal who absented himself from it would have his rations reduced by half" (40), "Napoleon, who was directing operations from the rear" (70), and "Napoleon had commanded that once a week there should be held something called a Spontaneous Demonstration" (77).

Major's control over language, over others, builds anticipation for further makers of words, for whom the play of tyrannical power is wordplay. The uncontested owners of language and its resources use their talent to serve strategies, with foregrounding attention to the teaching process, constructing student-animals as conformers to new ideologies: "The work of teaching and organizing the others fell naturally upon the pigs, who were generally recognized as being the cleverest of the animals" (9). The pigs have a "good" claim to leadership and privileges; a hierarchy already existed among the animals. Squealer is the best game player, in him we see nothing but convoluted words. Like Major, he can project his own mental linguistic images onto the minds of the underprivileged or onto the fabric of reality itself. Endowed with the quickest tongue, he shows a remarkable disposition for diversionary oratory—its incommunicable quality notwithstanding. He shares the deconstructionist's sense of free play in putting into the text what he regards as meaning: "He was a brilliant talker . . . he could turn black into white" (9). He is the apologist par excellence for the new corps of leaders. He slyly legitimates the exclusive consumption of the milk and apples by one of his palliatives, and he assigns noble motives to the pigs: "It is for *your* sake that we drink that milk and eat those apples" (23). It is testimony to his efficiency that he succeeds. This should not surprise us, for he is aware of and delights in his capability to incite, and takes advantage of the animals' linguistic vulnerability. His "eloquence [carries] them away" (35), and makes it doubtful that anyone would have an opposing thought. And to circumvent the possibility of this, he plays upon their variously scaled stresses—they are apprised of Jones's danger to them: "Do you know what would happen if we pigs failed in our duty? Jones would come back! . . . surely there is no one among you who wants to see Jones come back?" (23).

Malevolent Napoleon, though in character "not much of a talker" (9), still he adequately fits words and articulatory dynamics to objects. He offers to the perplexed animals a scapegoat to soothe other anxieties; pitch raising is used for additional reinforcement of persuasion: "'Comrades,' he said quietly, 'do you know who is responsible for this? Do you know the enemy who has come in the night and overthrown our windmill? SNOWBALL!' he suddenly roared in a voice of thunder, 'Snowball has done this thing!'". With the absence of Snowball which leaves no resistive voice, Napoleon establishes his reign by coercion. He retires into elitist isolation and rules by remote control. Squealer most effectively helps him by the instantaneously available speeches stating untruths throughout; language stands as a substitute for the status quo: "Do not imagine, comrades, that leadership is a pleasure! ... No one believes more firmly than Comrade Napoleon that all animals are equal ... And as to the Battle of the Cowshed, I believe the time will come when we shall find that Snowball's part in it was much exaggerated ... One false step, and our enemies would be upon us ... Once again this argument was unanswerable" (37). Ailing recognition of irrelevancy and inadequacy weighs the masses down. Squealer is a master manipulator of his approving listeners and his oratorical competence continues unabated throughout the novel. As economic shortages pile one on another, he placates them with fictionality masking as factuality. To the dunderheaded fools hearing is believing—particularly of scarcely remembered things—and familiarity has bred "understanding": "On Sunday mornings Squealer, holding down a long strip of paper with his trotter, would read out to them lists of figures proving that the production of every class of food-stuff had increased by two hundred per cent, three hundred per cent, or five hundred per cent, as the case might be. The animals saw no reason to disbelieve him, especially as they could no longer remember very clearly what conditions had been like before the Rebellion" (61–62). The reader gasps with wonder at Squealer's blatant absurdities. Claims and plain truth, signifiers and concrete reality, are widely disparate. The mass disinformationist wraps himself in the cloak of statistics. His freely inventive handling of numbers, woven in the very fabric of his discourse, dodges and goes unchallenged. Numbers have almost magical powers; they dissolve any doubt.

Squealer's quite heated verbalization, expanding into a narrative, about the death of Boxer banishes any disbelief over outrageous incongruities (83). He has had much practice in verbal acrobatics. In using hard vocabulary, distractors, he makes the content of the text as intransparent and distancing as possible: "This, said Squealer, was something called tactics. The animals were not certain what the word meant" (39). He never feels obliged to prove the case for legibility or for logical justification. Animals are caught in his semantic nets; they cannot decipher the complexities of arcane jargon and meaningless sound structures: "... it had been found necessary to make a readjustment of rations (Squealer always spoke of it as a 'readjustment', never as a 'reduction') ... Reading out the figures in a shrill rapid voice, he proved to them in detail that they had more oats, more hay, more turnips than they had in Jones's day ... The animals believed every word of it" (75). The finite minds of the animals are inherently incapable of the linguistically rich mind of Squealer; words do not fail him to take them further in: "You did not suppose, surely, that there was ever a ruling against *beds*? ... The rule was against *sheets*, which are a human invention" (45–46). Squealer is typically quick with indigenous diction that is not part of the animals' lexicon. Language becomes so opaque that it parodies its communicative purpose: "The other animals were too ignorant to understand. For example, Squealer told them that the pigs had to expend enormous labours every day upon mysterious things called 'files,' 'reports,' 'minutes' and 'memoranda'" (86). If the animals are left guessing about what happened, Squealer strikes out into further explanation that leaves them mute—their memory is viewed askance. On the issue of trading with the neighboring farms, Squealer "assured them that the resolution against engaging in trade and using money had never been passed, or even suggested" (43).

The propagandist's ability to transmute reality into linguistic artefacts, with such certainty of composure, is displayed in further situations. One such scene is that in which Squealer inflatedly attacks Snowball, tarnishing his name. He is baulked by Boxer who cannot grasp what he hears—Snowball "fought bravely at the Battle of the Cowshed. I saw him myself. Did we not give him 'Animal Hero, First Class'?" But Squealer is adamant; with customary ease he can write or unwrite a text, and Boxer's remark is brushed aside: "That was our mistake, comrade. For we know now—it is all written down in the secret documents that we have found—that in reality he was trying to lure us to our doom" (54). And if Boxer responds to sense rather than to the untruth-filled words, his unbending trust in the infallible Napoleon immediately impels him to silence: "If Comrade Napoleon says it, it must be right." When Snowball speaks falsely of the outcome of the battle, Boxer once again interrogates—he cannot see a victory as the windmill was demolished. Squealer's riddling phrases, however, confiscate disbelief (71). The passage from "Beasts of England" to the song of Minimus is unjustifiable to animals, but the commentator-at-large is "perspicacious" and interprets *raison* in this: "'Beasts of England' was the song of the Rebellion. But the Rebellion is now completed" (59).

In addition to the labyrinthine flow of words in which the rhetor indulges, he employs a language of physical gestures, bearing a false freight of emotional overtone. This emerges conspicuously in his explanation of the death of Boxer, where, amid a breakup of utterance, he affects sadness in a seemingly partisan manner: "Lifting his trotter and wiping away a tear ... Squealer's demeanor suddenly changed. He fell silent for a moment, and his little eyes darted suspicious glances from side to side before he proceeded ... he cried indignantly, whisking his tail and skipping from side to side" (83). This wordless language of communication has been used rather more crudely earlier by Major. Too conscious of making a speech he solemnly clears his throat twice (37), which raises an expectation of a high point in the paternalistic exhortation.

A secondary character who also drugs the masses with words beyond their ability to fathom is Moses. Like Squealer, he is what he is because of what he says than what he does. The clerically attired black raven gladly follows any leader, claiming a future happiness beyond the grave. He flies after an exiled Jones, then returns to the farm to be rewarded with "a gill of beer a day" (79) for his palliatives to the problems of real life circumstances—devaluing the here-and-now in favour of the everafter. His presence provides a scathing satire on religion. Being a raven, he is attracted to the odor of carrion on which he feeds, a verbal pun showing us the extent of Orwell's antipathy to religious symbolic expressions as organs of mass deception. As is the case with other successful orators, his use of a special diction and style, lacking semantic clarity, conveys a sense of authoritarian paternalism, which then puts his addresses in a credulous frame of mind.

The inflated rhetoricity of porcine texts is reinforced by the implications of the gradual lexical reformulation of Commandments, statutory, and inscriptions, in which the pigs, the appropriative authors and determinants of this text of texts, initially placed so much faith. Their success in scrambling it stems from their linguistic talent which deludes and obfuscates. As the Commandments are largely incomprehensible to the animals, Snowball "solves" the problem by conjuring a reducibly comprehensive label: "four legs good, two legs bad," an oversimplification, like the rest of the pigs' ideology, which disguises the evil intentions of the unscrupulous. Abridgement is the first step towards perversion. Birds find it hard to concur with Snowball's "judicial" analysis of their identity. Snowball exploits his linguistic superiority and silences their subtle questioning by his unintelligible proof that a wing "should therefore be regarded as a leg" and not as a "*hand*, the instrument with which he [man] does all his mischief" (22). By a verbal sleight of hand, he misreads the signifier and makes the bird appear quadruped. The pigs void the Commandments of their determinate and objective content—rendering the constant variable and the impermissible permissible by interpolating new tags: "'No animal shall sleep in a bed *with sheets*,' 'No animal shall kill any other animal *without cause*,' 'No animal shall drink alcohol *to excess*,' 'Four legs good, two legs better!' 'ALL ANIMALS ARE EQUAL BUT SOME ANIMALS ARE MORE EQUAL THAN OTHERS'" (45, 61, 73, 89, 90). This textual variation can be seen in the light of Paul Ricoeur's observation: " . . . a linking together of a new discourse to the discourse of the text."[3] The pigs exploit their listeners' lack of facility for recall, and their textual-comparison ineptitude. They emphasize the rhetorical basis of interpretation and discredit the denotative, univocal, and hermeneutical. In effect it would appear that they are deconstructors: they put in question the assumption that interpretation defines a stable and unquestionable truth about the Commandments.

It is remarkable that whilst most of the animals are able to make out letters and words, they cannot make the move toward meaning and semantic perception. Their learning disabilities are articulate in the reading and writing priming passage: "The dogs learned to read fairly well, but were not interested in reading anything except the Seven Commandments. Muriel, the goat, could read somewhat better than the dogs . . . Benjamin could read as well as any pig, but never exercised his faculty. So far as he knew, he said, there was nothing worth reading. Clover learnt the whole alphabet, but could not put words together. Boxer could not get beyond the letter D . . . Mollie refused to learn any but the five letters which spelt her own name . . . None of the other animals on the farm could get further than the letter A" (20–21). The passage charts the extent of the primates' verbal learning repertoire, their variable pacing, and endemic inequality. Some are less or more able than others. Classes prepare the dogs, who act as a punishing squad, for a particular reading task: to watch over the seven fundamental dogmas in which they have been indoctrinated. It is doubly ironic that the dog, well armed with powerful physique and canine teeth, is in fact the proverbial man's best friend. As the pigs eventually turn into "men," tyrannical humans, this largely offers itself as a verbal pun on the proverb. Benjamin has achieved poorly owing not to mental laziness to read texts but to his self-protective obtuseness. He is the linguistic anti-Squealer. The status quo seems to justify his pose of noninvolvement. His attitude which supposes the vacuity of the text (or life) comes close to the claim of deconstruction, the most radical of skepticisms about the text. This is evident from his quip "Donkeys live a long time. None of you has ever seen a dead donkey" (19). His own silent text will remain basically unchanged until Boxer is taken off to his death. A mood of defiance takes hold of him: "It was the first time that they had ever seen Benjamin excited—indeed it was the first time that anyone had ever seen him gallop. 'Quick, quick!' he shouted. 'Come at once! They're taking Boxer away!'" (81). Here Benjamin also speaks through nonverbal forms. This is a moment of revelation when a flat character suddenly, as a result of a more positive concern, outgrows his flatness. It is ironic that he reads without fail the sign on the knacker's van, since he prefers not to read. But his reaction is one that makes the whole situation more tragic. Realistic enough to see the writing on the wall for the rebellion before it starts, and always tongue-tied, it must therefore be an immense tragedy to bring him out of his cynical silence and to make him genuinely saddened. His subsequent response is definitive, it vents all the hate pent up for years of oppressed life. He abandons self-preservation in the face of this disaster. Benjamin thus seems to be a representation of Orwell himself. Orwell is the outspoken critic of communism after an intolerable, close view of the inner working of the system. On the other hand, Orwell could be seen as a betrayed Boxer, belatedly kicking his legs against the walls of the knacker's van, having been robbed of his power by his loyalty to the pigs.

Boxer's learner's ability stops at the infancy stage. His talent is taken up with ebullient physical activities emanating from a determinedly high sense of responsibility to the community and dedication to the work ethic. He suffers from great deficiencies in both episodic and semantic memory as well as in perceptual recognition. His illiteracy, we know, will be his undoing as he is carted off in the van and is ignorant of the markings on its side. Mollie, although not categorized low in words, but vain as she is, stops at decoding the five letters forming her name. The rest of the animals—the sheep, hens, and ducks—rank very low in achievement, almost unteachable. It cannot be a matter of surprise that the sheep identify with a communal ideology which makes them merge with the mass at the expense of individual autonomy. Put through a catechism, they become mere prattlers, finely tuned to pigs' ways. They loudly proclaim their unshakable loyalty by ritually breaking into "Four legs good, two legs bad" drowning any possibility of antiphonal thought.

This allows us to conclude that animals' learning disabilities will impede all efforts to improve their lot. They have the common man's responsibility in propping up tyrannies, and inviting their own victimization, through a trio of handicaps: a linguistic and cognitive deficiency, gullibility in acceptance of maneuverings at face value, and historical amnesia. However, there are a few oblique hints that the animals are not merely mindless beasts. They do have minds, they do think as we read that "they reasoned" (78), and that they have "the thought that at least he [Boxer] had died happy" (84), they also remember the issue of the pension field (85). This makes their betrayal all the more poignant since they are aware (if only obliquely) of what is happening to them.

One may ask whether it makes any sense to represent all animals as a single community. Can a mass society divided by a wide range of linguistic variation and differences in intelligence, among others, be said to hold a single doctrine? Pan-animalism cannot be a reality. It becomes apparent at the end of the novel that the pigs have firmly secured their position. The inference is that a shadow of doubt is thrown on a second insurrectionary round as long as the linguistic oligarchy will sustain their exploitation of the animals through the monopoly of language. If animals are ever to be liberated, they should be raised up into language and provided with semantic space to enable them to be conversant with the pigs and to engage them on their own ground with a counter discourse and gestures of their own.

The reader is indeed not wholly dependent upon the narrator's discourse for access to the characters. We should not be at all astonished to see that the narrator is totally coldly uncritical where tragic happenings take place. At Boxer's betrayal and at the cataclysmic massacre, extremely emotional contexts, his language is notably restrained. He ventures nothing, and soon after each event Squealer appears, attuning animals to mutability, constructing his versions of events, and explaining that what happened was justified, or what they just saw was not what really occurred. Indeed, there is a comic element in all of Squealer's presentations. The comic also appears in Orwell's attention to details. Out of context the idea that a pig on hind legs, wiping "hot" tears from his eyes in memory of a "departed" friend, is absurd. But here juxtaposed against an act of extreme betrayal, it assumes a very sinister note. Orwell's very silence and detachment would seem to carry much weight here, it is in such marked contrast to the agitation that crowds about. To add insult to injury, the pigs get drunk on whisky, paid for by Boxer's killing, on the night of his death. Though this is to be expected from the callous pigs, what makes this situation so black is that the animals do not connect Boxer's death with the pigs' drinking. Orwell's silence mirrors the animals' inability to discern truth.

A final point remains. Of some interest is Orwell's intertextual perspective which draws on his familiarity with and taste for Oriental materials. Language abets religious association which is, of course, burlesque. One detects nuances of the maximum number of wives permissible by Islam in Napoleon's "four sows [that] had all littered about simultaneously, producing thirty-one young pigs between them" (75). There is a clear injunction in the Holy Qur'an: " . . . marry women of your choice, two, or three or four; but if you fear that you shall not be able to deal justly [with them], then only one."[4] In a similar vein, the lush farm of the afterlife, where earthly suffering will be recompensed, shows intertextual possibilities and Orwell's attraction to Islamic epistemology. A heavenly "Sugarcandy Mountain" as envisioned by Moses is plentiful of material benefits for all animals: "It was situated somewhere up in the sky, a little distance beyond the clouds, Moses said. In Sugarcandy Mountain it was Sunday seven days a week, clover was in season all the year round, and lump sugar and linseed cake grew on the hedges" (10–11). This evokes the description of Paradise in the Holy Qur'an: "[There is] a Parable of the Garden which the righteous are promised: in it are rivers of water incorruptible; rivers of milk of which the taste never changes; rivers of wine, a joy to those who drink; and rivers of honey pure and clear. In it there are for them all kinds of fruits" (XLVII:15). Furthermore, Moses "even claimed to have been there on one of his higher flights, and to have seen the everlasting fields of clover and linseed cake and lump sugar growing on the hedges" (78)—a clear parody of Prophet Muhammad's ascent through the seven heavens [the night journey]: "Glory to [God] who did take his servant for a journey by night from the Sacred Mosque to the Farthest Mosque, whose precincts We did bless" (XVII:I). This contextual echo helps to keep us aware of the religious dimensions of Moses's titillating language.

Notes

1. In his essay "Why I Write," Orwell states that "good prose is like a window pane." *The Collected Essays, Journalism and Letters of George Orwell*, ed. Sonia Orwell and Ian Angus (London: Secker and Warburg, 1968) I:7.

2. George Orwell, *Animal Farm* (Penguin, 1989 edition) 1. All subsequent references will be to this edition and will be made parenthetically in the text.

3. See David M. Rasmussen, *Mythic-Symbolic Language and Philosophical Anthropology: A Constructive Interpretation of the Thought of Paul Ricoeur* (The Hague: Maritnus Nijhoff, 1971) 144.

4. *The Glorious Qur'an*, translation and commentary by Abdullah Yusuf Ali (The Muslim Students' Association of the United States & Canada, 1975) IV: 3.

V.C. LETEMENDIA

Revolution on Animal Farm: *Orwell's Neglected Commentary*

In the last scene of George Orwell's "fairy tale," *Animal Farm*, the humbler animals peer through a window of the farmhouse to observe a horrible sight: the pigs who rule over them have grown indistinguishable from their temporary allies, the human farmers, whom they originally fought to overthrow.[1] The animals' fate seems to mirror rather closely that of the common people as Orwell envisaged it some six years before commencing *Animal Farm*: "what you get over and over again is a movement of the proletariat which is promptly canalized and betrayed by astute people at the top, and then the growth of a new governing class. The one thing that never arrives is equality. The mass of the people never get the chance to bring their innate decency into the control of affairs, so that one is almost driven to the cynical thought that men are only decent when they are powerless."[2] Obviously *Animal Farm* was designed to parody the betrayal of Socialist ideals by the Soviet regime. Yet it has also been interpreted by various readers as expressing Orwell's own disillusion with any form of revolutionary political change and, by others, as unfolding such a meaning even without its author's conscious intention. It is time now to challenge both of these views.

Orwell himself commented of *Animal Farm* that "if it does not speak for itself, it is a failure."[3] The text does indeed stand alone to reveal Orwell's consistent belief not only in democratic Socialism, but in the possibility of

From *Journal of Modern Literature* 18, no. 1 (Winter 1992): 127–37. © 1992 by Indiana University Press.

a democratic Socialist revolution, but there is also a considerable body of evidence outside *Animal Farm* that can be shown to corroborate this interpretation. The series of events surrounding its publication, and Orwell's own consistent attitude towards his book provide evidence of its political meaning.[4] Meanwhile, of the two extant prefaces written by Orwell, the one designed for the Ukrainian edition, composed in 1947, is of particular political interest.[5] Orwell's correspondence with his friends and acquaintances on the subject of *Animal Farm* provides a further source of information. Some of these letters are well known to Orwell scholars, but his correspondence with Dwight Macdonald, with whom he became friends when he was writing for the American journal, *Partisan Review*, does not appear to have been fully investigated. Macdonald himself raised a direct question about the political intent of *Animal Farm* and was given a specific answer by Orwell, yet this fascinating evidence has apparently been neglected, in spite of the generous access now available to his correspondence in the Orwell Archive.[6]

Commentators on Orwell find it easy to conclude from *Animal Farm* the utter despair and pessimism either of its author, or of the tale itself.[7] It must be remembered, however, that through his allegory Orwell plays a two-sided game with his reader. In some ways, he clearly emphasizes the similarities between the beasts on Animal Farm and the humans whom they are designed to represent; at other times, he demonstrates with both humor and pathos the profound differences separating animal from man—differences which in the end serve to limit the former. In doing so, he forces his reader to draw a distinction between the personalities and conduct of the beasts and those of the human world. Of course, the animals are designed to represent working people in their initial social, economic, and political position in the society not just of Animal Farm but of England in general. The basic antagonism between working class and capitalist is also strongly emphasized by the metaphor: pig and man quarrel fiercely at the end of the story. The diversity of the animal class, like the working class, is equally stressed by the differing personalities of the creatures. Just because all have been subjected to human rule, this does not mean that they will act as a united body once they take over the farm. The qualities which, for Orwell, clearly unite the majority of the animals with their human counterparts, the common working people, are a concern for freedom and equality in society and a form of "innate decency" which prevents them from desiring power for any personal gain. While this decency hinders the worker animals from discovering the true nature of the pigs until the final scene, it also provides them with an instinctive feeling for what a fair society might actually look like. Yet Orwell was obviously aware, in using this metaphor, that the animals differ fundamentally from their human counterparts. Unlike men, the majority of the beasts are limited naturally by their brief lifespan and the consequent shortness of their memory. Moreover, their differentiated physical types deny them the versatility of humans. Their class structure is fixed by their immutable functions on the farm: a horse can never fill the role of a hen. The class structure of human society, in contrast, is free from such biological demarcations. These two profoundly limiting aspects of the animal condition, in which men share no part, finally contribute to the creatures' passivity in the face of the pig dictatorship. The metaphor, then, cannot be reduced to a simple equivalence, in the way that the pigs reduce the seven Commandments of Animal Farm to one.[8]

Evidently the animals lack education and self-confidence in spite of the active role which most of them played in the first rebellion and, in the case of some, are naturally stupid. Orwell is not implying by this the hopelessness of a proletarian revolution: he rather points to the need for education and self-confidence in any working class movement if it is to remain democratic in character. Both of these attributes, he appears further to suggest, must come from within the movement itself. The crude proletarian spirit of the common animals necessarily provides the essential ingredient for a revolution towards a free and equal society, but it needs careful honing and polishing if it is not to fall victim to its own inherent decency and modesty. If this simple, instinctive decency is to be preserved in the transition from revolution—which is all too easy—to the construction of a new society—which is not—other kinds of virtue are also necessary and must at all costs be developed by the working class if it is not to be betrayed again. The text itself, however, hints at disaster for the rule of the pigs. Their single tenet asserting that some animals are more equal than others is in the end a meaningless absurdity. In spite of their great intellectual gifts, the pigs are ultimately the most absurd of all the farm animals, for they are attempting to assume a human identity which cannot belong to them. It is left to the reader to ponder the potential for political change, given the evident weakness and vanity at the core of the pig dictatorship. The final scene of the book, moreover, reveals the disillusionment of the working beasts with their porcine leaders, an essential step in the process of creating a new revolution.[9]

Evidence external to the text of *Animal Farm* is not required to establish the political meaning within its pages. Yet an examination of Orwell's attitude towards the book during the difficult period in which he tried to have it published only strengthens the conclusions drawn here. Even before *Animal Farm* was finished, Orwell was quite aware that it would cause controversy because of its untimely anti-Stalinist message, and he predicted difficulties in publishing it.[10] He was, of course, correct: the manuscript was refused by Gollancz, Andre Deutsch, and Jonathan Cape—in the latter case on the advice of the Ministry of Information. Meanwhile, Orwell declined an offer to publish the book in serial form in Lady Rhondda's *Time and Tide*, explaining that the politics of the journal were too right-wing for his tale, only to be turned down by T.S. Eliot at Faber and Faber, his next choice of publisher. The end of the story is well known to Orwell scholars: Orwell went finally to Frederick Warburg, who accepted the manuscript, and upon its publication in August 1945, it was well received and soon selected by the Book-of-the-Month Club.[11] Orwell's interest in the major publishing houses, as well as his reluctance to approach Frederick Warburg as a first choice and his willingness at one desperate point to pay himself to have the work reproduced in pamphlet form show that he wanted it to reach the public at all costs and to address as wide an audience as possible from as unprejudiced a political context as he could find. Naturally, Lady Rhondda's journal would not have been suitable: his purpose was not to congratulate conservatives or even liberals on the failure of the Russian Revolution, however scathing his criticism of the Stalinist regime within the allegory. Furthermore, Orwell stood firmly against any suggested alterations to the text, particularly in the instance of his representation of the Bolsheviks as pigs. He made no excuses for *Animal Farm*—as he would in the case of *Nineteen Eighty-Four*—and must have considered its message to be fairly clear, for he offered no press releases to correct misinterpretations of the book from either right- or left-wing political camps.[12] On the contrary, it rather seems that he was proud of the quality, as much as the political timeliness, of the book and expected it to require no external defence or explanation; this opinion did not appear to change.[13]

Some further indication of Orwell's own view of *Animal Farm* may be found in the two prefaces he wrote for it. Of the two, only the Ukrainian preface was actually published. Its original English version, written early in 1947, has never been found, and only a translation from the Ukrainian is available to Orwell scholars. This presents the possibility that various errors or subtle alterations of meaning might have remained uncorrected by the author when it was first translated from English to Ukrainian.[14] Written two years after the English preface, the Ukrainian piece obviously betrays a purpose very different from that of its predecessor, as a result supplying the reader with far more direct commentary on the text. Orwell makes it clear here that he "became pro-Socialist more out of disgust with the way the poorer section of the industrial workers were oppressed and neglected than out of any theoretical admiration for a planned society." His experiences in Spain, he states, gave him first-hand evidence of the ease with which "totalitarian propaganda can control the opinion of enlightened people in democratic countries." Not only were the accusations against Trotskyists in Spain the same as those made at the Moscow trials in the USSR; Orwell considers that he "had every reason to believe that [they] were false," as far as Spain was concerned. Upon his return to England, he discovered "the numerous sensible and well-informed observers believing the most fantastic accounts of conspiracy, treachery and sabotage which the press reported from the Moscow trials." What upset him most was not the "barbaric and undemocratic methods" of Stalin and his associates, since, he argues, "It is quite possible that even with the best intentions, they could not have acted otherwise under the conditions prevailing there." The real problem, in his view, was that Western Europeans could not see the truth about the Soviet regime, still considering it a Socialist country when, in fact, it was being transformed "into a hierarchical society, in which the rulers have no more reason to give up their power than any other ruling class." Both workers and the intelligentsia had to be disabused of this illusion which they held partly out of wilful misunderstanding and partly because of an inability to comprehend totalitarianism, "being accustomed to comparative freedom and moderation in public life." To make possible, then, a "revival of the Socialist movement" by exposing the Soviet myth, Orwell writes that he tried to think of "a story that could be easily understood by almost everyone and which could be easily translated into other languages."[15]

He claims that although the idea came to him upon his return from Spain in 1937, the details of the story were not worked out until the day he "saw a little boy, perhaps ten years old, driving a huge cart-horse along a narrow path, whipping it whenever it tried to turn." If the horse could only become aware of its own strength, the boy would obviously have no control over it. Orwell found in this a parallel with the way in which "the rich exploit the proletariat," and he proceeded from this recognition "to analyse Marx's argument from the animals' point of view." For them, he argues, the idea of class struggle between humans was illusory; the real tension was between animals and men, "since whenever it was necessary to exploit animals, all humans united against them." The story was not hard to elaborate from this, Orwell continues, although he did not actually write it all out until 1943, some six years after the main ideas had been conceived of. Orwell declines to comment on the work in his preface, for "if it does not speak for itself, it is a failure." Yet he ends with two points about details in the story: first, that it required some chronological rearrangement of the events of the Russian Revolution, and, second, that he did not mean pigs and men to appear reconciled completely at the end of the book. On the contrary, "I meant it to end on a loud note of discord, for I wrote it immediately after the Teheran Conference [parodied by the final scene in *Animal Farm*] which everybody thought had established the best possible relations between the USSR and the West. I personally did not believe that such good relations would last long. . . ."[16]

It seems, then, that as much as Orwell wanted to explain how he had arrived at Socialism and at his understanding of totalitarianism, he sought to indicate in this preface to Ukrainian readers how workers and intelligentsia in Western Europe, but especially in England, misperceived the difference between the Soviet Union of 1917 and that of twenty and thirty years later. *Animal Farm* was, according to its author, an attempt to strip away the mythical veil shrouding the Stalinist regime; simultaneously, however, he was trying to renew what had been lost through this deception and to revive the original spirit of the Socialist movement. It seems possible to conclude that Orwell is suggesting the presence of just such a double intention within the allegory. One point in the preface, however, requires clarification. Orwell's reference to the animals' view that the real class struggle lay between animals and humans suggests, in the context of the allegory, the absence of any significant class struggle between members of the ruling class—or humans—since they will readily forget their differences and unite to oppress animals. This appears confusing when applied to Marx's theory, which Orwell claims as the theoretical basis of this insight, and furthermore it does not capture the thrust of the story itself, in which the divisions between animals are exposed in detail, rather than those between humans, or even between humans and animals.[17] But Orwell makes it quite clear here that he refers to an animal perspective in defining the class struggle as one between humans and beasts. Certainly the point of departure was, in both the Russian situation and in this particular allegory, the identification and removal of the most evident class of oppressors. In this initial movement, the oppressed class was not mistaken politically; what came afterwards in both instances, though, demonstrated that the first movement of revolutionary consciousness had not been sustained in its purity, since the goals of the revolution gradually began to be violated. Orwell's remark in the preface that "[f]rom this point of departure [the animals' view of the class struggle], it was not difficult to elaborate the rest of the story" cannot be taken as an admission that the animals' perspective was perfectly correct.[18] Of course, the book debunks such a simplistic interpretation of the class struggle, in spite of its initial accuracy.

By revealing the divisions within the animal ranks, Orwell is cautioning his reader to question the animal view of the class struggle, for the crucial problem that even the wise Old Major does not predict in his identification of the real enemy is the power-hunger of the pigs. By allegorical implication, this points rather interestingly to Orwell's identification of a flaw in the Marxian theory of revolution itself. Although its starting point is clearly the animals' partially accurate but insufficient analysis of the class struggle, the allegory in its course reveals more and more drastically the inadequacy of such a view as a basis for post-revolutionary society. Part of Old Major's vision is indeed debunked, while the truth of the initial insight about class struggle is never denied, and the story, as has been seen, ends on a note of hope. Orwell's final point in the preface constitutes the only correction and very mild apology that he would make about the text, even though he had had roughly two years to assess the critical response—and hence the variety of misinterpretations—circulating about *Animal Farm*. Here he is warning his reader about the subtlety of his allegory: pigs and humans may come to look the same at the end, but they are still essentially enemies and share only a greed for power. For it is indeed the dispute between farmers and pigs which completes the transformation of pig to man and of man to pig.

If the Ukrainian preface was written for an unknown audience, the English preface was designed for readers with whom Orwell was much more familiar. Written in 1945, when he was still bitterly upset over the difficulties of printing unpopular political commentary in wartime Britain, the English preface is concerned not with the content of the story but with the question of whether he would be free to publish it at all because of current political alliances, intellectual prejudices, and general apathy over the need to defend basic democratic liberties.[19] Attacking as he does here the political toadying of the Left intelligentsia in Britain to the Stalinist regime, Orwell presents *Animal Farm* as a lesson for the well-educated as much as the uneducated.[20] Meanwhile, the fact that he makes no reference in this preface to the details of the book indicates his strong confidence in its political clarity for English readers, although his bitter tone shows, as Crick suggests, Orwell's acute sense that he was being "persecuted for plain speaking" before *Animal Farm* was published.[21] Since the English preface does not actually offer an interpretation of *Animal Farm* explaining Orwell's political intention, it is necessary to look for this information in his more private communications on the subject.

Orwell commented explicitly on his book to his friends Geoffrey Gorer and Dwight Macdonald. Crick states that Orwell gave a copy of *Animal Farm* to Gorer having marked in it the passage in which Squealer defends the pigs' theft of the milk and apples. He told Gorer that this "was the key passage."[22] This emphasis of Orwell's is reiterated and explained more fully in a letter to Dwight Macdonald written shortly after *Animal Farm* first appeared in the United States, in 1946. Macdonald was one of a group of American intellectuals who had broken with Soviet Communism as early as 1936 and had gone to work with Philip Rahv and William Phillips on *Partisan Review*.[23] From January 1941 to the summer of 1946, Orwell had sent regular "letters" to the review and had had cause to correspond with Macdonald fairly frequently. Macdonald was later to move to the editorship of *Politics*, described by Orwell in a letter to T.S. Eliot as "a sort of dissident offshoot" of *Partisan Review*, and had already championed a review written by Orwell that had been rejected for political reasons by the *Manchester Evening News*.[24] This shared political understanding soon developed into a literary friendship which lasted until Orwell's death in 1950.[25]

In September 1944, Orwell had already written to Macdonald expressing his views about the Soviet Union. Given that only a few months separated the completion of *Animal Farm* from this letter, it seems safe to assume that the views expressed in both might be similar. To Macdonald, Orwell stated, "I think the USSR is the dynamo of world Socialism, so long as people believe in it. I think that if the USSR were to be conquered by some foreign country the working class everywhere would lose heart, for the time being at least, and the ordinary stupid capitalists who never lost their suspicion of Russia would be encouraged." Furthermore, "the fact that the Germans have failed to conquer Russia has given prestige to the idea of Socialism. For that reason I wouldn't want to see the USSR destroyed and think it ought to be defended if necessary." There is a caution, however: "[b]ut I want people to become disillusioned about it and to realise that they must build their own Socialist movement without Russian interference, and I want the existence of democratic Socialism in the West to exert a regenerative influence upon Russia." He concludes that "if the working class everywhere had been taught to be as anti-Russian as the Germans have been made, the USSR would simply have collapsed in 1941 or 1942, and God knows what things would then have come out from under their stones. After that Spanish business I hate the Stalin regime perhaps worse than you do, but I think one must defend it against people like Franco, Laval etc."[26]

In spite of its repressive features and its betrayal of basic human freedoms, then, Orwell still considered the Soviet regime to be vital as an example to the working class everywhere. The real danger lay in the idea that it defined Socialism. What was most needed was a new form of democratic Socialism created and maintained by the people. He offers meanwhile the possibility that such democratic forms of Socialism elsewhere might actually have a benign effect on the Russian regime.[27] In the allegorical context of Animal Farm, Napoleon's dictatorship would still seem to be a step forward from that of the human farmers—according to Orwell's letter, the rule of "the ordinary stupid capitalists." For animals outside the farm, it would provide a beacon of hope—so long as the truth about the betrayal taking place within was made plain to them. For it would now become their task to build their own movement in a democratic spirit which might, in Orwell's words, "exert a regenerative influence" on the corruption of the pigs' realm.

When *Animal Farm* finally appeared in the United States in 1946, Macdonald wrote again to Orwell, this time to discuss the book: "most of the anti-Stalinist intellectuals I know ... don't seem to share my enthusiasm for *Animal Farm*. They claim that your parable means that revolution always ends badly for the underdog, hence to hell with it and hail the status quo. My own reading of the book is that it is meant to apply to Russia without making any larger statement about the philosophy of revolution. None of the objectors have so far satisfied me when I raised this point; they admit explicitly that is all you profess to do, but still insist that implicit is the broader point. . . . Which view would you say comes closer to your intentions?"[28]

Orwell's reply deserves quoting in full: "Of course I intended it primarily as a satire on the Russian revolution. But I did mean it to have a wider application in so much that I meant that that kind of revolution (violent conspiratorial revolution, led by unconsciously power-hungry people) can only lead to a change of masters. I meant the moral to be that revolutions only effect a radical improvement when the masses are alert and know how to chuck out their leaders as soon as the latter have done their job. The turning point of the story was supposed to be when the pigs kept the milk and apples for themselves (Kronstadt). If the other animals had had the sense to put their foot down then, it would have been all right. If people think I am defending the status quo, that is, I think, because they have grown pessimistic and assume there is no alternative except dictatorship or laissez-faire capitalism. In the case of the Trotskyists, there is the added complication that they feel responsible for events in the USSR up to about 1926 and have to assume that a sudden degeneration took place about that date, whereas I think the whole process was foreseeable—and was foreseen by a few people, e.g. Bertrand Russell—from the very nature of the Bolshevik party. What I was trying to say was, 'You can't have a revolution unless you make it for yourself; there is no such thing as a benevolent dictatorship.'"[29]

Yes, *Animal Farm* was intended to have a wider application than a satire upon the Russian regime alone. Yes, it did indeed imply that the rule of the pigs was only "a change of masters." Yet it did not condemn to the same fate all revolutions, nor for a moment suggest that Farmer Jones should be reinstated as a more benevolent dictator than Napoleon. According to Orwell's letter, the problem examined by *Animal Farm* concerns the nature of revolution itself. Unless everyone makes the revolution for him or herself without surrendering power to an elite, there will be little hope for freedom or equality. A revolution in which violence and conspiracy become the tools most resorted to, one which is led by a consciously or unconsciously power-hungry group, will inevitably betray its own principles.[30] Failing to protest when the pigs kept the milk and apples for themselves, the other animals surrendered what power they might have had to pig leadership. Had they been "alert and [known] how to chuck out their leaders"[31] once the latter had fulfilled their task, the original spirit of Animal Farm might have been salvaged. The book itself, Orwell makes clear in his letter, was calling not for the end of revolutionary hopes, but for the beginning of a new kind of personal responsibility on the part of revolutionaries. The most important barrier in the way of such a democratic Socialist revolution was the Soviet myth: if people outside still thought that that particular form of revolution could succeed without betraying its goals, nothing new could be accomplished. The final note of Orwell's letter is optimistic: if people mistook his message for a conservative one, it was precisely their problem. They had no confidence in the possibility of an alternative to either capitalism or dictatorship. In a sense, they would be like those animals who, when forced into making a choice between a false set of alternatives by Squealer—either the return of Farmer Jones or unquestioning obedience to the rule of the pigs—failed to consider the possibility of a third choice, a democratic Socialist society. For although Orwell was prepared to provide a fairly detailed explanation of his animal story for his friend Macdonald, his letter makes it quite evident that the burden of understanding *Animal Farm* still lay with its reader.

Given the striking congruity between the text and Orwell's political commentary about it, it would be rash to argue that he had lost control of his allegory in *Animal Farm*. If it takes time and effort to expose the political intricacies behind the stark prose of his animal fable, this must have been partly his intention: the lesson of democracy was not an easy one to learn, and the next revolutionary move towards democratic Socialism could surely not be allowed to repeat the mistakes of Old Major. Still, we may wonder if the grain of hope provided by the final scene of the book is not, in this light, too insubstantial to feed a new generation of revolutionaries. Yet if Orwell had presented an easy political resolution to the horrors of totalitarianism, his warning would lose its force. His reader could remain complacent, detached from the urgent need for personal involvement in political change so emphasized by the animal allegory. If he had designed a political solution for the other beasts, furthermore, he could be accused of hypocrisy: his whole argument both inside and outside the text rested on the proposition that the people had to make and retain control of the revolution themselves if they wanted it to remain true to its goals. The deceit of the pigs was not the only failure on Animal Farm, for the foolish simplicity of the other animals and, indeed, of Old Major's naive idea of revolutionary change were as much to blame for the dictatorship which ensued. Orwell had to warn his readers that their apathy and thoughtlessness were as dangerous as blind admiration for the Stalinist regime. Only when all members of society saw the essential need for individual responsibility and honesty at the heart of any struggle for freedom and equality could the basic goals of Socialism, as Orwell saw them, be approached more closely. Meanwhile, no single revolutionary act could create a perfect world, either for the animals or for the humans whom they represent in the story. Acceptance of the notion of class struggle could not lead to an instant transformation of society unless those who would transform it accepted also the difficult burden of political power, both at the time of and after the revolution. While the most corrupting force on Animal Farm was the deception practiced upon the other animals by the pigs, the greatest danger came from the reluctance of the oppressed creatures to believe in an alternative between porcine and human rule. Yet it was in the affirmation of dignity, freedom, and equality tacitly provided by the nobler qualities of the presumed lower animals that Orwell saw the beginnings of such an alternative. So it is that, in the last moment of the book, he leaves open the task of rebuilding the revolution on a wiser and more cautiously optimistic foundation.

Notes

1. George Orwell, *Animal Farm* (Harcourt Brace, 1946), p. 118. Further references to the text are to this edition and are given parenthetically.

2. Sonia Orwell and Ian Angus, eds., *The Collected Essays, Journalism and Letters of George Orwell* (Penguin, 1971), Vol. I, p. 372. (This four-volume collection will be referred to henceforth as *CEJL*). Even when Orwell wrote this, in deep distress after his experience of the Spanish Civil War, he was not completely pessimistic, as he remarked with some surprise: see *Homage to Catalonia* (Penguin, 1984), p. 220.

3. *CEJL*, III, p. 459.

4. Much of Orwell's other writing, particularly that which is contemporary to the creation of *Animal Farm*, also supports the interpretation offered here. See, for example, *CEJL*, III, pp. 83 and 280–82; "Tapping the Wheels," *Observer*, 16 January 1944, p. 3. This is not to mention Orwell's radical writings of the earlier war years, exemplified by his revolutionary enthusiasm in *The Lion and the Unicorn* (see *CEJL*, II, pp. 74–134) and his two essays for Gollancz' *The Betrayal of the Left* (1941), "Fascism and Democracy" and "Patriots and Revolutionaries" (pp. 206–14 and 234–45). After *Animal Farm*, Orwell's position remained unchanged; see, for example, "The British General Election," *Commentary*, November 1945, pp. 65–70, and "What Is Socialism?" *Manchester Evening News*, 31 January 1946, p. 2.

5. For the Ukrainian preface, see *CEJL*, III, pp. 455–59; see also "The Freedom of the Press," *The Times Literary Supplement*, 15 September 1972, pp. 1036–38.

6. The author would like to thank the staff of the Orwell Archive, University College, University of London for their very kind assistance in searching out the relevant materials for this discussion, as well as for their help in finding resources for the larger work on Orwell's politics of which it is but a small part. She would like to thank the estate of the late Sonia Orwell and Martin Secker & Warburg for permission to publish extracts from their collection of Orwell's correspondence. She would also like to thank the Yale University Library for permission to publish extracts from the Dwight Macdonald Papers and for its generosity in making available to her copies of other letters in their Manuscripts and Archives collection. This article was obviously accepted for publication (28 March 1990) before

the appearance of Michael Shelden's *Orwell: the Authorized Biography* (Heinemann, 1991). Shelden's thorough research uncovered the Macdonald correspondence, quotations from which were employed for the purpose of biographical, rather than political, analysis.

7. See, for example, Patrick Reilly, *George Orwell: the Age's Adversary* (Macmillan, 1986), pp. 266–67; Alan Sandison, *George Orwell: After 1984* (Macmillan, 1986), p. 156; Alok Rai, *Orwell and the Politics of Despair* (Cambridge University Press, 1988), pp. 115–16; Stephen Sedley, "An Immodest Proposal: Animal Farm," *Inside the Myth* (Lawrence & Wishart, 1984), p. 158; and Alex Zwerdling, *Orwell and the Left* (Yale University Press, 1984), pp. 90–94.

8. A full discussion of the animal–human metaphor and its political purpose is not within the scope of this brief study, but is elaborated upon fully in the author's doctoral dissertation, "'Free from Hunger and the Whip': Exploring the Political Development of George Orwell" (University of Toronto, 1992).

9. Raymond Williams, in his *George Orwell* (Viking, 1971), shares this view: see pp. 74–5.

10. Bernard Crick, *George Orwell: a Life* (Penguin, 1980), p. 450; for an indication of Orwell's own fears about the unpopularity of his book, see *CEJL*, III, pp. 71–2, 118–19 and 168–70.

11. For a full account of the publication problems and the reception of *Animal Farm*, see Crick, pp. 452–58 and pp. 487–90.

12. For an account of Orwell's own criticism of *Nineteen Eighty-Four*, the conditions under which it was written, and the statement which he issued in order to correct political misinterpretations of it, see Crick, pp. 546–51 and 565–70.

13. For evidence of his apparent satisfaction with the book, see *CEJL*, I, p. 29. His friend William Empson recalls him complaining when the book first appeared that "'not one of [the reviews] said it's a beautiful book.'" See Audrey Coppard and Bernard Crick, eds., *Orwell Remembered* (BBC, 1984), p. 183.

14. Peter Stansky and William Abrahams, in their *Orwell: the Transformation* (Granada, 1981), also consider this worth mentioning: see p.185. Peter Davison, at present in the process of editing *The Complete Works of George Orwell*, has already discovered a surprising number of mistakes or changes made during the past publication of Orwell's work in English: it seems logical that the potential inaccuracies of a re-translated translation uncorrected by its original author should be contemplated seriously. For a brief account of Davison's discoveries, see *The Sunday Times*, 2 March, 1986, p. 5.

15. *CEJL*, III, pp. 455–8.

16. *CEJL*, III, pp. 458–59.

17. Stephen Sedley concludes from this that "[t]he muddle is remarkable" and that "the book begins and ends by debunking" the idea of a class struggle between animals and humans, whether it be attributed to the animals or to Orwell himself (Sedley, p. 161). Rai, meanwhile, argues from the Ukrainian preface that "*Animal Farm* had been intended as an allegory of the common people, awaking to a realization of their strength and overthrowing their oppressors," but that "[i]n working out the fable, however, in the winter of 1943–4, the euphoria collapsed" (Rai, p. 115). Rai seems to forget Orwell's own comment at the beginning of the preface that the idea for *Animal Farm* was linked to his experience in Spain and explicitly designed to debunk the Soviet myth. This already suggests a story with a far from idyllic ending. It was only after the idea had been conceived of, according to Orwell, that

he decided on the details of the story. It would thus appear likely that Orwell had thought through the political message of his story long before the winter of 1943.

18. *CEJL*, III, p. 459.

19. "Freedom of the Press," pp. 1036–38.

20. Orwell considered that many such intellectuals had substituted for love of their own country a far more slavish regard for the Soviet Union. For his ideas on this issue, see "Notes on Nationalism," *CEJL*, III, pp. 410–31. In other writing of the time, his language was even stronger than that of the English preface: see, for example, p. 263.

21. Crick, p. 463. Orwell was not, however, the only writer to feel this: as his friend Arthur Koestler explains, "George and I were the only anti-Stalinists who could get printed. We felt we were persecuted by the *New Statesman* etc., and what appalled us was not just the refusal to print what we had written, but the systematic suppression of fact so that people simply did not know what was going on. Sources of truthful information were the privately circulated news sheets. . . . But people like Beaverbrook suppressed a great deal. I remember the 'Beaver' saying how we all liked 'Uncle Joe' and therefore mustn't say too much against him." (Coppard and Crick, eds., pp. 167–68).

22. Crick, p. 490. It is a pity that Crick does not provide here the source of this important information.

23. David Caute, *The Fellow Travellers* (Weidenfeld & Nicholson, 1973), pp. 88–9; see note. See also Crick, p. 392.

24. See letter from Orwell to T.S. Eliot, 5 September 1944 in the Orwell Archive, reproduced by kind permission of the estate of the late Sonia Orwell and Martin Secker & Warburg. For details of the rejected book review, see *CEJL*, III, pp. 169–70.

25. An indication of its depth is that Sonia Orwell, when first considering the possibility of contravening her husband's dying wish and authorizing a biography of him, wrote to Macdonald to see if he would undertake it. He accepted with enthusiasm, but she later withdrew her offer, having decided that it was too early for a biography to appear. See correspondence between Sonia Orwell and Dwight Macdonald in the Orwell Archive.

26. Letter from Orwell to Dwight Macdonald, 5 September 1944, Dwight Macdonald Papers, Manuscripts and Archives, Yale University Library; copy in Orwell Archive, reproduced by kind permission of the estate of the late Sonia Orwell and Martin Secker & Warburg. Orwell made a similar point in a later letter to Frank Barber, in which he states: "My attention was first drawn to this deliberate falsification of history by my experiences in the Spanish civil war. One can't make too much noise about it while the man in the street identifies the cause of Socialism with the USSR, but I believe one can make a perceptible difference by seeing that the true facts get into print, even if it is only in some obscure place." (15 December 1944, Orwell Archive), reproduced by kind permission of the estate of the late Sonia Orwell and Martin Secker & Warburg. At this date, of course, Orwell was still waiting for *Animal Farm* to "get into print"; it might be that his comment about "some obscure place" could refer to the book itself.

27. In another letter to Macdonald written at the time that Orwell was involved with his final novel, *Nineteen Eighty-Four*, he argues with an optimism which might surprise some of his critics: "Communism will presently shed certain unfortunate characteristics such as bumping off its opponents, and if Socialists join up with the

CP they can persuade it into better ways" (2 May 1948, Dwight Macdonald Papers, Manuscripts and Archives, Yale University Library; copy in Orwell Archive).

28. Letter from Dwight Macdonald to Orwell, 2 December 1946, Dwight Macdonald Papers, Manuscripts and Archives, Yale University Library; copy in Orwell Archive. The argument to which Macdonald objects is still a favorite with Orwell's critics on the Left: Stephen Sedley offers it in his critique of *Animal Farm* (Sedley, *op. cit.*).

29. Letter from Orwell to Dwight Macdonald, 5 December 1946, Dwight Macdonald Papers, Manuscripts and Archives, Yale University Library; copy in Orwell Archive. It is interesting to compare this statement with one made by Orwell in a commentary on Randall Swingler's *Violence* published in *Polemic*, V (September–October, 1946), pp. 45–53: "I do not believe in the possibility of benevolent dictatorship, nor, in the last analysis, in the honesty of those who defend dictatorship. Of course, one develops and modifies one's views, but I have never fundamentally altered my attitude towards the Soviet regime since I first began to pay attention to it some time in the nineteen-twenties. But so far from disappointing me, it has actually turned out somewhat better than I would have predicted fifteen years ago" (p. 53).

30. This is not to argue that Orwell defended pacifism; his fighting in Spain and his urgent and frequent attempts to join the army during the Second World War demonstrate his acceptance of the need for violent combat in order to defend basic human liberties. Yet he was evidently aware of the ease with which violence and conspiracy could be turned against the initial purpose which seemed to justify them. In the text of *Animal Farm*, Boxer's sorrow at the necessity of violence even in the struggle to overthrow human rule suggests a deeper wisdom than he is often given credit for (see pp. 36–7).

31. Letter from Orwell to Dwight Macdonald, 5 December 1946.

ROGER FOWLER

Animal Farm

Coming Up for Air, written in Morocco where Orwell and Eileen spent the winter of 1938–9, was published on 12 June 1939, just before the outbreak of the world war which its hero awaits; Orwell's next work of fiction, *Animal Farm*, was not written until November, 1943–February, 1944. The gap between the two books was unusual for Orwell. He had been publishing a book a year: the seven novels and documentary works which appeared between 1933 and 1939 . . . and a volume of essays, *Inside the Whale*, in April 1940. There seems to have been a conscious pause for reflection and planning in the early 1940s: in April, 1940, he wrote to Geoffrey Gorer that 'at present I am very anxious to slow off and not to hurry on with my next book, as I have now published 8 in 8 years which is too much'.[1] He said he was planning 'a long novel in three parts', of which the first was to be called either '*The Lion and the Unicorn*' or '*The Quick and the Dead*'.

Orwell and Eileen moved to London in May 1940: Eileen was working in the Censorship Department at Whitehall, Orwell was to work at the BBC from August 1941 to November 1943. He wrote reviews and journalism for *Time and Tide*, *Horizon*, *Partisan Review* and *Tribune*, of which he became Literary Editor on leaving the BBC.

The larger project no doubt continued to mature during this period of journalism and broadcasting, but the details of his thoughts and plans are, as

From *The Language of George Orwell*, pp. 159–80, 237–38. © 1995 by Roger Fowler.

usual with Orwell, not clearly available to us. In the autumn of 1940 he wrote three political essays, 'England your England', 'Shopkeepers at War' and 'The English Revolution' which were published in 1941, under the title *The Lion and the Unicorn: Socialism and the English Genius*, in the series 'Searchlight Books' edited by Tosco Fyvel and Orwell for Secker & Warburg. This is not the first volume of the fictional trilogy which he mentioned earlier as in prospect, but it could be considered the political preface in a series of three different books, of which the second volume was to be *Animal Farm* (a fable of the Russian Revolution) and the third *Nineteen Eighty-Four* (a dystopian vision of post-revolutionary totalitarianism in an imaginary future Britain).[2] Certainly he was planning *Nineteen Eighty-Four* long before he actually wrote it in 1946—as early as 1943, he said, and indeed an outline called 'The Last Man in Europe' exists in manuscript, probably from 1943.[3] (And as I have pointed out (p. 158 above), George Bowling's panic about the 'after-war' in *Coming Up for Air* (written 1938–9) presages themes of *Nineteen Eighty-Four* much earlier still.)

As Orwell took stock of his political ideas and his writing future after completion of *Coming Up for Air*, so we may at this point very briefly review his stylistic situation at the time. By the end of the 1930s, Orwell had established a voice of his own as a down-to-earth, serious yet witty essayist; he had also practised and mastered a range of more literary techniques appropriate to a certain kind of novel. His novels focus on the mind, feelings and development of the individual; always an individual whose relationship with the surrounding social, cultural and political world is problematic. Orwell has a variety of 'realistic' descriptive techniques for communicating the substance of the world in which the hero lives—Dorothy's Suffolk, Gordon Comstock's London, the battlefield in Spain—all requiring different techniques. He also, drawing much from Joyce, developed styles for the rendering of modes of thought and feeling, the mind-styles of these alienated individuals faced with the anxieties and guilts of colonialism, sex, modernity, technology. Orwell could be said to have developed a modernist style of novel in the spirit of Joyce and Lawrence, and a heightened language for the consciousness of his central characters. The characters also live and think in a language-rich world, realized by Orwell through the techniques of heteroglossia.

Orwell's last fiction, *Nineteen Eighty-Four*, continues with the modernist and heteroglossic strategies of his earlier work—*Aspidistra* and *Coming Up for Air* are particularly close to the last novel both thematically and linguistically. Before that, however, there comes *Animal Farm*, a beast fable of the Russian Revolution and its betrayal, written in the sparest linguistic style and more reminiscent of Swift than of Joyce. It is a radical stylistic departure for Orwell: to only a slight extent prepared for by his earlier linguistic experiments, and unique in the lucid simplicity of its prose.

Animal Farm is one of the most familiar books in world literature. It tells how the livestock and working animals at Manor Farm are given an account of a dream by Old Major, a prize Middle White Boar: 'a dream of the earth as it will be when Man has vanished' (p. 12). Major predicts an uprising of the animals against their owner, Mr Jones, and this happens three months later. Meanwhile the leading pigs, Napoleon and Snowball, and their spokesman Squealer, elaborate Major's ideas into a system of thought which they call 'Animalism', based on the principles of equality among the animals, and avoidance of the vices of humankind. After the overthrow of Jones, the animals run the farm cooperatively, but gradually the pigs take more and more tyrannical control and assume the vices of humanity; they deprive the other animals of proper sustenance, and of a say in the running of the farm; they engage in foolish grandiose projects, principally the building of a windmill;[4] they trade and consort with human beings; they kill. At the end the pigs have become men, the other animals are in their customary state of oppressed deprivation. The wheel has come full circle.

The fable exists quite clearly and coherently on two beautifully matched levels, and in this clarity and system lies the secret of its success. At the first level, it is a story about the fabulous human-like deeds of farm animals, their triumphs and their ultimate betrayal and failure: this is the level at which the story's charm has been enjoyed by generations of young readers. Orwell's principal source was surely the section of Swift's *Gulliver's Travels* (1726) in which Gulliver travels to the land of the Houyhnhnms, a race of benevolent horses who rule their own society with the humans or Yahoos in a role of servitude. But the beast fable is in fact much older, a classical genre dating at least from the Greek fables of 'Aesop' of the fifth century BC,[5] in which the sayings and deeds of animals represent human moral dilemmas. Orwell's animal 'fairy story' (as he subtitled it) encompasses the whole range of farm animals. Some are individualised, others treated *en masse*. Characterisation is slight, but focused and consistent, and draws more on our existing stereotypes of types of beast than on elaborate portrayal in the book. For example, rightly or wrongly, pigs have a bad name for selfishness and gluttony, and that is their image in this text; similarly, the dogs are vicious but fawning, the cat self-centred and crafty, the donkey bad-tempered; the two carthorses Boxer and Clover are slow-witted, strong, gentle and loyal; the sheep are brainless and behave as a flock without any individual initiative. Although the farm animals think and talk, do the work of humans and to some extent use tools, nothing really outrageous or fantastic, nothing out of the nature of their species, is attributed to them. The narrator is at pains to describe the difficulties encountered by the animals in farming and building: they cannot use any tool which requires standing on two legs, and therefore have to break up the stone for the windmill by dropping it; a pig climbs a ladder with difficulty; a brush or chalk is held between the knuckles of the trotters, cows are milked in the same way, and so on. That which is natural or easy for the animals is also mentioned, e.g. weeding is much more efficient under their regime than when done by humans, because the animals are naturally equipped to browse; grains of corn and scraps of hay are collected without waste by the hens and ducks with their sharp eyes and well-adapted beaks. At the animal-story level of reading, the reader will be curious about how such practicalities are accomplished, and the text encourages and gratifies this curiosity. What is more, the text secures the reader's empathy with the animals by techniques of focalisation which stick close to their interests and expectations, as we will see.

The above should be expressed, however, not in terms of all the animals, but of 'animals-except-pigs'; the thoughts, speech and behaviour of the pigs are treated in an alienated, grossly human, manner (cf. Swift's distasteful portrayal of the Yahoos). In the case of the pigs, who appropriate the leadership and exploit their power against the interests of the other animals, their nature is humanly perverted as they speak in the voice of political rhetoric and duplicity, and are gradually transformed into a grotesque parody of human beings as they take to selling and buying, drinking alcohol, wearing clothes and walking on their hind legs. At the level of the text as animal story, then, the reader's engagement in the account of a gradual division between oppressors and oppressed is guided by appropriate language for the two groups, with, as we will see, a narrator's style very close to that of the group of the majority, the betrayed innocents, the horses, sheep, fowl, etc.

The story of oppression, betrayal and suffering is carried in parallel on the second level, the level of political allegory. Everyone except the child reader knows that the beast fable is also a satire on a real, historical, narrative of revolution betrayed. Orwell uses the animals to present an evaluation of the events and personalities of the Soviet Union from the 1917 Revolution to the Stalinist purges of the 1930s and the Teheran Conference of 1943, with a condemnation of the techniques of Soviet totalitarianism, particularly the falsification of history and reality by a wilful perversion of language. There is a close correspondence of the characters and incidents in *Animal Farm* with Soviet communism and its sources: thus, 'Major' represents Marx, 'Napoleon' Stalin, 'Snowball' Trotsky, the windmill represents the first Five-Year Plan of 1928, the meeting of pigs and humans at the end represents the Teheran Conference—the meeting between Stalin, Roosevelt and Churchill—and so on. These correspondences have been recovered and charted in detail by previous commentators on *Animal Farm*.[6] The satire on the Soviet Union was too direct for several publishers to whom Orwell first offered the book—after all, Russia was still at that time a wartime ally. Moreover, hostile critics of the political Left objected that in attacking Soviet Communism Orwell was abandoning his apparently firmly established socialist beliefs. These objections miss Orwell's intentions—although it must be admitted that the book itself does not make these intentions clear. In his preface to the Ukrainian edition of *Animal Farm*, written in 1947, Orwell explains that he was attacking Soviet Communism not simply for itself, but because he wanted to attack the Soviet *myth* as received in Britain, where it was harmful to the Socialist movement (*CEJL*, III, pp. 455–9). He also wrote that the book 'is intended as a satire on dictatorship in general'.[7] Misinterpretation of *Animal Farm* has arisen largely because of the simplicity of its language, in particular, the extreme lightness of touch of the narrative style, its refusal to offer any strong direct evaluation of the events of the fable. As William Empson, poet and expert on ambiguity, advised Orwell, 'the danger of this kind of perfection is that it means very different things to different readers'.[8] One pertinent fact about the book is that, because of its imaginative coherence, it can impart pleasure and moral significance to readers who do not recognize the Soviet references: the story and its values exist independent of the historical allegory. But it is equally obvious that the politically naive reading will miss Orwell's essential purpose and its satirical expression. It is not just an animal story, but a fiction which, indirectly and by literary techniques, makes a political statement about dictatorship. As Orwell noted in 'Why I Write,' '*Animal Farm* was the first book in which I tried, with full consciousness of what I was doing, to fuse political purpose and artistic purpose into one whole' (*CEJL*, I, p. 29).

Narrative Style in *Animal Farm*

All the critics agree on the simplicity of the language in *Animal Farm*, and that it is unique in the canon of Orwell's writing. If we take George Woodcock (Orwell's friend, and author of a fine critical study) as representative, we find him speaking of 'this crystalline little book', 'conciseness of form and simplicity of language', 'a bare English, uncluttered by metaphor,' a style 'direct, exact and sharply concrete,' 'a series of lively visual images held together by a membrane of almost transparent prose'.[9] Woodcock and other critics also stress how different the spare, neutral prose is from the styles achieved in Orwell's other fiction. As we saw, Orwell had developed a 'demotic' idiolect which, while vernacular in vocabulary, is hardly cool or neutral, rising often to heights of rhetoric and stridency. When we looked at descriptive aspects of Orwell's writing, we found that his prose is less often as clear 'as a window pane', more often decorative and emotive or symbolic. And as far as fictional narration is concerned, we have seen that the narrator's voice is strongly foregrounded in the other books, so much so that one compositional problem which Orwell had to solve in the 1930s was the toning-down of the Orwellian narrative persona and its replacement by a character's focalisation. *Animal Farm* represents the ultimate reduction in the status of the narrative voice, which is extremely impersonal, but in this book it is not displaced by the viewpoint of a *single* character, as with John Flory, Gordon Comstock or George Bowling; in *Animal Farm* Orwell creates a sort of *collective* focalisation, as we will see in the next section.

It is vital to relate the linguistic simplicity of *Animal Farm* to a second context. Not only is it a technical departure from Orwell's stylish and experimental earlier fiction and from his more exuberant essay writing, the style of *Animal Farm* is also an outcome of a new phase of his thinking about the politics and morality of language usage. In Chapter 3 I gave an account of Orwell's views on language, detailing in particular the position which emerged in the first half of the 1940s. He analysed the ills of political speech and writing, which in his view resulted in the self-deception and lying which were the intellectual preconditions for totalitarianism. The period of gestation and writing of *Animal Farm* coincides with the development of his new focus on the morality of public language; and a major theme of the book is the perversion of language by an oppressive dictatorship. The simplification, one might even say purification, of his own language in *Animal Farm* no doubt reflects his desire for linguistic honesty in political writing, and is the foil against which the degradation of language by the pigs is presented. His six-point programme for good usage (reproduced on p. 34 above) goes a long way to describing the practical measures which he followed in simplifying and clarifying the narrative voice in *Animal Farm*.[10]

As a basis for understanding the language of *Animal Farm*, let us first try to make sense of the usual observations that its narrative style is 'impersonal' and 'simple.' Note that to some extent this will involve saying that certain linguistic features are *not* present. . . .

The opening pages of *Animal Farm*, like all good fictional openings, set the tone and therefore illustrate many of the points that need to be made:

> Mr Jones, of the Manor Farm, had locked the hen-houses for the night, but was too drunk to remember to shut the pop-holes. With the ring of light from his lantern dancing from side to side, he lurched across the yard, kicking off his boots at the back door, drew himself a last glass of beer from the barrel in the scullery, and made his way up to bed, where Mrs Jones was already snoring.

As soon as the light in the bedroom went out there was a stirring and a fluttering all through the farm buildings. Word had gone round during the day that old Major, the prize Middle White boar, had had a strange dream on the previous night and wished to communicate it to the other animals. It had been agreed that they should all meet in the big barn as soon as Mr Jones was safely out of the way. Old Major (so he was always called, though the name under which he had been exhibited was Willingdon Beauty) was so highly regarded on the farm that everyone was quite ready to lose an hour's sleep in order to hear what he had to say.

At one end of the big barn, on a sort of raised platform, Major was already ensconced on his bed of straw, under a lantern which hung from a beam. He was twelve years old and had lately grown rather stout, but he was still a majestic-looking pig, with a wise and benevolent appearance in spite of the fact that his tushes had never been cut. Before long the other animals began to arrive and make themselves comfortable after their different fashions. First came the three dogs, Bluebell, Jessie, and Pincher, and then the pigs who settled down in the straw immediately in front of the platform. The hens perched themselves on the window-sills, the pigeons fluttered up to the rafters, the sheep and cows lay down behind the pigs and began to chew the cud. The two cart-horses, Boxer and Clover, came in together, walking very slowly and setting down their vast hairy hoofs with great care lest there should be some small animal concealed in the straw. Clover was a stout motherly mare approaching middle life, who had never quite got her figure back after her fourth foal. Boxer was an enormous beast, nearly eighteen hands high, and as strong as any two ordinary horses put together. A white stripe down his nose gave him a somewhat stupid appearance, and in fact he was not of first-rate intelligence, but he was universally respected for his steadiness of character and tremendous powers of work. After the horses came Muriel, the white goat, and Benjamin, the donkey. Benjamin was the oldest animal on the farm, and the worst tempered. He seldom talked, and when he did it was usually to make some cynical remark—for instance, he would say that God had given him a tail to keep the flies off, but he would sooner have had no tail and no flies. Alone among the animals on the farm he never laughed. If asked why, he would say that he saw nothing to laugh at. Nevertheless, without openly admitting it, he was devoted to Boxer; the two of them usually spent their Sundays together in the small paddock beyond the orchard, grazing side by side and never speaking. (*Animal Farm*, pp. 5–7)

Let us begin with syntactic simplicity. Sentences are never very short (thus avoiding an oral, clipped effect) nor very long (avoiding bookishness). Their typical syntax is a sequence of short phrases and clauses paratactically strung together, with meaning packaged in short information units:

With the ring of light/ from his lantern/ dancing from side to side,// he lurched across the yard,// kicking off his boots/ at the back door,// drew himself a last glass of beer/ from the barrel/ in the scullery,// and made his way up to bed,// where Mrs Jones was already snoring.

Clauses are typically active, transitive, with a human or animal subject performing a simple action in a location or on an object:

Subject	Verb	Object or location
Mr Jones	had locked	the hen-houses
	shut	the pop-holes
he	lurched	across the yard
	kicking off	his boots
	drew	a last glass of beer
	made his way	up to bed
Mrs Jones	snoring	
other animals	began to arrive	
pigs	settled down	in the straw
hens	perched	on the window-sills
pigeons	fluttered	up to the rafters
sheep and cows	lay down	behind the pigs
	chew the cud	
cart-horses	came in	
	walking	
	setting down	hoofs

and so on. The active, transitive pattern of Subject, Verb, Object (SVO) is particularly noticeable in passages describing sequences of actions such as the 'battle of the cowshed'.

There is a noticeable lack of adjectives throughout the whole text, with the exception of single, simple descriptive and identifying adjectives: 'strange dream', 'big barn', 'raised platform', 'enormous beast', etc. There is a related avoidance of complex noun phrases: 'vast hairy hoofs' with two adjectives is as complex as we get in this opening passage. Complex noun phrases, particularly those with adjectives and qualifying phrases both before and after the central noun, take a lot of processing, and, like hypotaxis, connote an intellectual complexity which is inappropriate to the focalisers of this story.

Turning to the idea that *Animal Farm* is 'impersonal' in manner, it is obvious that this effect is achieved by eliminating those linguistic markers which suggest the presence of 'a personal voice' or a dominating narrator. One effect of this abstinence is that the book's narrative discourse contains no first-person pronouns, neither singular ('I', 'me', 'my') referring to a narrative persona, nor plural ('we', 'us', 'our') appealing to a community of views or experiences among readers or any other group external to the text. There are no stereotypical generalisations, no references to 'those kinds of . . .'. The few present-tense general statements are extremely modest in their claims: 'it is not easy for a pig to balance himself on a ladder', p. 23). There is no invocation of a reader, no dialogism. Moreover, the text is absolutely parsimonious as far as modality is concerned, avoiding terms which typically signal judgement or evaluation—'may', 'should', etc., and making very few comments of any kind. The remark on the carthorse, Boxer, is very typical of what Orwell's narrator permits himself in this respect:

> A white stripe down his nose gave him a somewhat stupid appearance; and in fact he was not of first-rate intelligence, but he was universally respected for his steadiness of character and tremendous powers of work.

To whom did he appear stupid, and by whom was he universally respected? The judgement does not go beyond what the other animals might think of their colleague. Orwell generally avoids any claim of knowledge or opinion which might be felt to be external to the animals' world. The following aside is about as far as he strays outside the bounds of what they would know; Snowball tells the animals that electricity produced by the windmill will drive various machines:

> The animals had never heard of anything of this kind before (for the farm was an old-fashioned one and had only the most primitive

machinery), and they listened in astonishment while Snowball
conjured up pictures of fantastic machines ... (p. 44)

The animals would not know that the farm was 'old-fashioned' and its
machinery 'primitive', because they have no comparison: here then is a
very slight hint of a viewpoint different from and more knowledgeable
than theirs.

We turn now to the character of the vocabulary and its contribution
to the narrative style. The basic vocabulary register is plain and simple, concrete and domestic: 'drunk', 'lurched', 'kicking off his boots', 'glass of beer',
'scullery', 'snoring'. There are plenty of colloquial idiomatic phrases such as
'safely out of the way', 'got her figure back'. Understandably, there are many
ordinary words relating to farm equipment and procedures, and to animals:
'hen-houses', 'pop-holes', 'tushes', 'perched', 'fluttered' 'chew the cud'; 'harness-room', 'stables', 'bits', 'nose-rings', 'dog-chains', 'knives', 'castrate', 'reins',
'halters', 'blinkers', etc. (p. 20). The prevalence of this type of vocabulary
gives the text an old-fashioned pastoral air which accords well with Orwell's
nostalgia for an older rural England. Some words seem to be deliberately
archaic, typically the word 'muted' (p. 37) which has been noticed by other
commentators: it refers to pigeons defecating on the heads of the humans in
the battle of the cowshed. Other traditional terms, less noticeable, are found
here and there: 'cartage' (p. 43), 'governess-cart' (p. 54), 'clamps', 'chaff',
'mangels' (p. 65).

The ordinariness of the dominant vocabulary links the narrative style of
Animal Farm with Orwell's earlier 'demotic' register, but there are important
differences. Orwell's demotic in the essays, *Down and Out*, and the second
part of *Wigan Pier*, for example, is heightened into an instrument of personal
rhetoric or naturalistic description by sordid references, by vulgarisms and
swear words, by emotive, negative and hyperbolic adjectives. *Animal Farm*
avoids these populist and expressive gestures, but remains resolutely controlled, mundane and low-key in its lexical register. It is also virtually free of
any obvious metaphor: the dancing light in the opening paragraph (which is
entirely functional) is exceptional. And there are no elaborate, laboured simi-
les, foreign words or jargon. Orwell was clearly following the programme for
linguistic plainness and conceptual clarity which he was to set out in 'Politics
and the English Language'.

We will shortly consider how the everyday vocabulary of *Animal Farm*
relates to focalization in the fable. There is one further observation to make on
vocabulary, however, and that concerns the rather conspicuous use throughout the text of a slightly 'higher' level of vocabulary than the mundane lexis
of farmyard affairs. 'Ensconced' in the opening sequence is more striking than

most words in this register, to which I would add the more typical 'communicate', 'highly regarded', 'wise and benevolent', 'not of first-rate intelligence', 'universally respected'. The vocabulary in question is somewhat elevated, a bit formal and staid; not showy or literary, but slightly more proper and educated than one would associate with the animals. Some more examples: 'vivacious', 'inventive', 'degrading', 'positive pleasure', 'parasitical', 'light skirmishing manoeuvre', 'impromptu celebration', 'under the superintendence', 'a conciliatory message', 'point of honour'.

Focalisation, Empathy and Distance

From whose point of view is the story told? What has been said in the previous section about the impersonality of the narrator's voice, and the plainness of the narrative's diction, suggests that Orwell subdues any appearance of a separate story-teller with his own knowledge and opinions. He knows as much as the animals know—perhaps, in terms of farming and building technique, a bit more—but there is no privileged, God-like knowledge which would set the narrator above or apart from the animals. There is no version of the Orwell-figure (either narrator or character) that appears in every other book by our author. Basically, focalisation is from the point of view of the animals; but this statement needs to be made a little more precise.

The distinction between *internal perspective* and *external perspective* . . . applies to the present book; and the distinction is used to express a division of empathy. The villains in the moral scheme—principally the pigs, but also the dogs, Moses the raven, and Mollie the vain horse who defects—are externally presented. (The same applies to the humans.) Their physical appearance and reputation are stressed, their motives are never explored. They are how they appear to others, and they are potentially grotesque from the outset:

> The best known among them was a small fat pig named Squealer, with very round cheeks, twinkling eyes, nimble movements, and a shrill voice. He was a brilliant talker, and when he was arguing some difficult point he had a way of skipping from side to side and whisking his tail which was somehow very persuasive. The others said of Squealer that he could turn black into white. (*Animal Farm*, pp. 15–16)

Napoleon, the pig who takes control after the expulsion of Snowball, is never seen from the inside, though his dictatorial decisions run the greater part of the plot. A good example would be his role in the sale of some timber, in which he produces a highly confusing, rumour-filled atmosphere eventuating in his betrayal by Frederick (the allegorical representative of Hitler): we are never shown his motives and reasons, though his actions, assumed titles and appearance are presented in a number of ludicrous images in the same chapter (Chapter 8). Later, when the pigs take to drinking, further comic images are generated:

> At about half past nine Napoleon, wearing an old bowler hat of Mr Jones's, was distinctly seen to emerge from the back door, gallop rapidly round the yard, and disappear indoors again. (p. 92)

The grotesque treatment of the pigs is progressive. Their physical traits are at the outset individuating, but the grotesquerie of the bodies is more and more emphasised until finally, standing on their hind legs and wearing clothes, they have become men-monsters. And all the time we hear nothing of their thoughts—though, as we will see, we hear a lot of their speech.

Orwell's way of referring to the actors in this beast-drama constantly insists on a distinction between 'the pigs' and 'the animals'. 'The animals' are basically horses, cows, sheep, hens and ducks, and they are described, as Hammond puts it 'as if from the inside'.[11] Four are named, and of these only two, the horses Boxer and Clover, are assigned anything in the way of individual thought and feeling. That they are animals, rather than human characters in a novel, makes it seem natural that they receive no depth or complexity of psychological presentation, but the horses are allowed feelings and motives. Boxer's reactions to events are communicated throughout:

> 'His answer to every problem, every setback, was "I will work harder!"—which he had adopted as his personal motto'

> 'he decided to be content with the first four letters' of the alphabet

> 'He is dead. . . . I have no wish to take life'

> 'Boxer, who had now had time to think things over, voiced the general feeling'

> 'Boxer would never listen to her'

and so on. He is a stereotype of faithful loyalty and hard work; his 'motherly' colleague Clover embodies care and pathos, and is treated to an extended account of deep, sorrowful feeling after the murderous purges begin (pp. 75–6).

Boxer and Clover are to a large extent representatives of the primary focalisation of the animals, which is *collective*: the horses 'voice the general feeling'. Scores of clauses throughout the book give their actions, reactions and feelings as a group; the following are typical:

The singing of this song threw the animals into the wildest excitement.

they were so delighted with the song

the animals hated Moses

the animals could hardly believe in their good fortune

all the animals capered with joy

[the animals] gazed round them

All the animals nodded in complete agreement

Now if there was one thing that the animals were completely certain of

The animals had their breakfast

the animals trooped down to the hayfield

The animals were happy

the animals were completely certain.

The animals had now reassembled in the wildest excitement

the animals decided unanimously

the animals crept back into the barn

the animals were dismayed

the animals did not want Jones back

the animals were somewhat surprised

There are countless other examples of this sort of structure. Three things may be noticed about them. First, they are generally in the simple active syntax which was observed in the style of the narrative frame (of course they are technically part of that frame); the simplicity, it seems to me, reflects on the psychological and moral straightforwardness of the members of this category 'animals-except-pigs'. Second, the vocabulary displays the kind of domestic, rural, modesty which we have noticed; it is very rare that the slightly more elevated diction is associated with the animals' experiences—'every mouthful of food was an acute positive pleasure' (p. 26) is an exceptional instance of incongruity of register. Third, these formulaic clauses between them hold the content of the animals' world of experience and behaviour: they encode animal actions, sensations, emotions, knowledge and doubts. In fact, they establish the primary focalisation of the tale: they ensure that the story is told from the viewpoint of the animals. And because these focalisation-clauses are conveyed in the basic style of the narration itself, empathy between the narrator and the animals-except-pigs is established.

There is also, of course, the slightly elevated register which we have noticed, which is proper to the narrator and not to the animals: the function of this hint of a more experienced and literate perspective is to keep open the possibility of detachment. Though Orwell sympathises with the animals and their suffering under the tyranny of the pigs, he maintains a slight distance. They are naive and gullible, too ready to blame themselves when the pigs tell them that their memory is defective. Orwell allows us to perceive these realities and not be dominated by the 'reality' which is falsely experienced by the animals. This distance is helped by an affectionately humorous tone in which the animals are presented. There are comic scenes to lighten this dark narrative: the Battle of the Cowshed is a choreography of animal antics; the bleating sheep are comic and so is the silliness of Mollie the vain horse.

The Rhetoric of Dominance and the Perversion of Language

One feature of this disastrous animal utopia is a marked disproportion in the allocation of language to the various classes of animal. Success in language relates directly to the amount of power enjoyed by the different species: power to understand the processes of farming and of government, power to control the fates of other species. The pigs learn to read and write fluently, the others learn less well, their success diminishing according to the conventional stereotypes of their intelligence: Orwell analyses their relative attainments in detail (pp. 29–30), constructing the descending hierarchy pigs–donkey–goat–dogs–horses–sheep–hens–ducks. Their different commands of language correspond roughly to their degrees of control over their lives in this new regime.

There is a marked difference in the amounts of *speech* assigned to the different animals. Except for one small oration by Pilkington at the end, humans do not speak, though their rumours and plots are to some small extent reported. All the rest of the animals are imagined to have speech, though as far as the lower orders go, this seems to be limited to confessing crimes, and these confessions are reported, not direct. In the early days the animals participate in debates, but their contributions (other than those of the pigs) are reported rather than direct speech. Only the horses, the goat and the donkey hold conversations, and then in a very limited way, and—scanning the text as a whole—surprisingly rarely, at least in direct speech (pp. 16, 39, 41, 60, 70, 71–2, 74–5, 77 (one word!), 88, 90, 101, 103–4, 114).

Not surprisingly, dominance by speech is exercised by the pigs. There are four speakers among them: Major, who delivers a long Marxist exhortation on exploitation and rebellion; Napoleon, the Stalin-like leader for most of the narrative; Snowball, who is expelled by Napoleon; and Squealer, who is the intermediary and spokesman for Napoleon's regime and has by far the most speech in the book. Language as deployed by these speakers has different roles, but together their speech makes up *Animal Farm*'s version of the 'voices of the other' which appear regularly in Orwell's writing. Against the mundane, familiar language in which the story and the animals' experiences are narrated, the pigs' speech stands out as an alien linguistic world, half laughable but ultimately chilling. It exemplifies the 'swindles and perversions' of English which Orwell analysed in 'Politics and the English Language', and which are a constant butt for parodic attack in his later writings—there is a sketch of political speech in *Coming Up for Air* (Part Three, chapter 1), parodies of the writings of the intelligentsia in 'Politics and the English Language', and of course this mode of linguistic satire is fully developed in *Nineteen Eighty-Four*.

Major's long speech (pp. 7–12) is a set-piece parody of, in general terms, political demagoguery, and specifically, the discourse of theoretical Marxism. It is not, however, excessive in its manner—jargon is rare, sentences are not over-elaborate, emotive terms are controlled. As the mainspring of the story, presented as the intervention which encourages the animals to rebellion when opportunity arises, this speech must be experienced as if it was persuasive at the time: not outrageous, comic, or incomprehensible through extreme distance from the animals' register. It begins in a plain serious mode, with the experienced public speaker's careful signposting of the way he is going to organise his oration, and a calculated note of pathos:

'Comrades, you have heard already about the strange dream that I had last night. But I will come to the dream later. I have something

else to say first. I do not think, comrades, that I shall be with you
for many months longer, and before I die, I feel it my duty to pass
on to you such wisdom as I have acquired.'

Although initially subdued, the speech is immediately dialogic: Major
foregrounds himself as the authoritative 'I', and gathers his audience as
'Comrades': he is going to maintain a controlled focus on and appeal to his
listeners, because his intention is to implicate them in his reasoning and
persuade them to action. 'Comrades' and 'you' recur throughout the speech.
After the preliminaries, the rhetoric shifts up a gear:

'Now, comrades, what is the nature of this life of ours? Let us face
it: our lives are miserable, laborious, and short. We are born, we are
given just so much food as will keep the breath in our bodies, and
those of us who are capable of it are forced to work to the last atom
of our strength; and the very instant that our usefulness has come
to an end we are slaughtered with hideous cruelty.'

The dialogic dimension continues to be prominent, designed to carry
the audience along by preempting their responses. Note the rhetorical question 'what is . . . ?', used throughout the speech: 'But is this simply part of the
order of nature?', 'Why then do we continue in this miserable condition?' etc.
Also contributing to the dialogic rhetoric is the pronoun 'we', used here as in
political discourse generally to imply community of interest and consensus
of belief.[12] As Major heightens the rhetoric after the calm opening, the style
becomes rhythmic, estranged from ordinary speech by organisation of the
syntax into three-part structures (triads) which are typical of political oratory:
'miserable, laborious, and short'; 'born . . . food . . . work'. Vocabulary becomes
emotive: 'slaughtered with hideous cruelty'. Major begins to work with generalisations which suggest absolute certainty: 'No animal in England is free.
The life of an animal is misery and slavery: that is the plain truth.' Slogans
follow naturally: 'All men are enemies. All animals are comrades.' For all the
dignity of his style, and his scholastic analysis of production and consumption, Major is basically playing on the animals' feelings, and laying down the
law: the law consists of a set of declarations towards the end of his speech, the
basis of 'The Seven Commandments' which are later inscribed on the wall of
the barn (p. 23).

After the death of Major, and after the Rebellion, the law is determined
principally by Napoleon and Snowball, and then by Napoleon after Snowball's
expulsion. Napoleon uses language very differently from Major. He addresses
the animals rarely, and when he does, his speeches are 'short and to the point'

(p. 118). His decisions are communicated to the animals, along with other announcements and opinions which are necessary to regulating the animals' view of the world, by his garrulous spokesman Squealer. But although Napoleon has little direct speech in this narrative, his utterances are repeatedly summarised in forms which present them as instruments of great power. He is the source of a stream of what are called in linguistics *speech acts*:[13] utterances which, in being spoken, do not simply refer to some state of affairs in the world, but actually perform an action—in this case, Napoleon performs speech acts which coerce and control the animals. Some of the verbs which name these speech acts are:

> announced, read out the orders, abolished, dismissed, ordered, decreed, forbidden, pronounced a solemn decree, instructed, gave orders, delivering orders, laid down as a rule, commanded, pronounced a short oration, pronounce the death sentence, pronounced, issued his orders, accepted a contract, called upon, demanded

Napoleon decrees a state of affairs, Squealer announces it, 'explains' it, and the world of the animals is thereby changed—a procedure in which language is clearly both source and instrument of power.

It can be seen that language is of fundamental significance in *Animal Farm*, and in a number of respects. It is first of all the medium for narration, the telling of the tale, and in that role it has a specific stylistic character, which both models the mind-style of the animals (in its underlying mundane, pastoral simplicity) and slightly distances them (by the somewhat elevated narrator's register). When we look at the language of the pigs, comparing it both in quantity and in style with that associated with the other animals, we realise that language is also part of the *action* of the book, and that the relationship of language and power symbolised by linguistic actions is a theme examined by this fable. This theme becomes more specifically focused as the pigs' regime gets indefensibly brutal and selfish: language can be used in a perverted way in order to support a distorted, untruthful, version of reality. There is a hint of this in the first presentation of Squealer (quoted above) as a brilliant talker who 'could turn black into white'. This is precisely Squealer's role throughout the narrative, a role which he takes over from the banished Snowball. The Seven Commandments, initial moral code of Animalism, are by Snowball reduced for ease of memorisation by the animals (also to blur its details) to the maxim 'Four legs good, two legs bad' which even the dim-witted sheep can bleat enthusiastically. The text continues:

The birds at first objected, since it seemed to them that they also had two legs, but Snowball proved to them that this was not so.

'A bird's wing, comrades,' he said, 'is an organ of propulsion and not of manipulation. It should therefore be regarded as a leg. The distinguishing mark of Man is the *hand*, the instrument with which he does all his mischief.'

The birds did not understand Snowball's long words, but they accepted his explanation, and all the humbler animals set to work to learn the new maxim by heart. (*Animal Farm*, p. 31)

The long words stand out against the simpler language of the narrative, and are a patent grotesquerie of language by which Orwell mocks the lying logic of Snowball as Snowball squares the world with the maxim by redefining wings as legs. The animals, though handled sympathetically rather than patronisingly, are naive, and take in Snowball's explanation. It is Squealer who performs this function of redefining black as white for the animals for most of the story. When the pigs greedily claim the apple harvest for themselves, 'Squealer was sent to make the necessary explanation to the others': this is not done in a spirit of selfishness, but it has been proved by Science that apples are necessary to the pigs if they are to manage the farm and keep Jones from returning . . . (p. 32). Similarly he 'explains' many other deviations from the Commandments, and other illogicalities: for example, pp. 49–50, 52, 57—he 'set the animals' minds at rest. He assured them that the resolution against engaging in trade had never been passed'; p. 60 'he put the whole matter in its proper perspective'; when it is learned that the pigs are sleeping in beds, contrary to Commandment 4: 'The rule was against *sheets*'. At this point the alteration of language to falsify history, a great theme of *Nineteen Eighty-Four*, becomes explicit, for the Commandment is repainted on the barn wall: 'No animal shall sleep in a bed *with sheets*'. The horror and the historical revisions escalate: Commandment 6, 'No animal shall kill any other animal' is soon negated by the addition of 'without cause' after the murderous purges (p. 78). The narrator comments, with gentle irony, 'Somehow or other, the last two words had slipped out of the animals' memory.' Finally, all the Commandments, and thus the principles of the Rebellion, are erased, and replaced by a single Commandment which voices a self-contradictory 'justification' for the superiority of the pigs:

ALL ANIMALS ARE EQUAL
BUT SOME ANIMALS ARE MORE
EQUAL THAN OTHERS (p. 114)

The insane logic of this slogan is clearly within the domain of what Orwell was later to call 'doublethink', simultaneous belief in two contradictory propositions (see Winston Smith's account in *Nineteen Eighty-Four*, p. 35). Voiced in language, doublethink produces a stylistic shock—here, the blatant perversion of the meaning of the word 'equal', a key logical and ethical term. Semantic contradiction is found elsewhere in orders which are issued by the pigs to manage the other animals:

> Napoleon announced that there would be work on Sunday afternoons as well. This work was strictly voluntary, but any animal who absented himself from it would have his rations reduced by half. (p. 53)

> Napoleon had commanded that once a week there should be held something called a Spontaneous Demonstration. (pp. 97–8)

Forced spontaneity is part of Orwell's vision of the totalitarian future in *Nineteen Eighty-Four* (see p. 23). Also attacked in that novel are false announcements of productivity and rations, a topic which figures in *Animal Farm* too. Squealer's Sunday morning readings of trumped-up production figures may be noted (p. 79), but his announcement of a reduction in rations is more significant for language and doublethink:

> Once again all rations were reduced, except those of the pigs and dogs. A too rigid equality in rations, Squealer explained, would have been contrary to the principles of Animalism.

Note how the meaning of 'equality' is here eroded in preparation for the debasement of 'equal' in the final version of the Commandments. Squealer continues:

> For the time being, certainly, it had been found necessary to make a readjustment of rations (Squealer always spoke of it as a 'readjustment', never as a 'reduction'), but in comparison with the days of Jones, the improvement was enormous. (p. 95)

'Readjustment' for 'reduction' is, as narrated here, a pointed euphemism, precisely the kind of verbal dishonesty to which Orwell has sensitised us in a memorable paragraph of 'Politics and the English Language':

> In our time, political speech and writing are largely the defence of the indefensible. . . . Thus political language has to consist largely

of euphemism, question-begging and sheer cloudy vagueness. Defenceless villages are bombarded from the air, the inhabitants driven out into the countryside, the cattle machine-gunned, the huts set on fire with incendiary bullets: this is called pacification. (*CEJL*, IV, p. 166)

Notes

1. Quoted in Crick, *George Orwell: A Life* (London: Secker & Warburg, 1980) pp. 262–3.

2. Ibid, pp. 262–3 and 273. 'When he wrote *Animal Farm* and then *Nineteen Eighty-Four*, he must have assumed that people knew already where he stood politically, would recognise the assumptions behind his satires'.

3. The text is reproduced in the first edition of Crick, *Orwell*, pp. 407–9.

4. Windmills (arguably, grotesque objects in themselves) have popularly symbolised human delusion ever since Don Quixote jousted at one in Cervantes's tale *Don Quixote*, thinking it was a giant; hence the expression 'tilting at windmills' applied to someone who foolishly attacks a position which is a figment of his own imagination.

5. Aesop, *Fables*, trans. by S. A. Handford (Harmondsworth: Penguin, 1954).

6. See J. R. Hammond, *A George Orwell Companion* (London: Macmillan, 1982), pp. 160–2; Valerie Meyers, *George Orwell* (London: Macmillan, 1991) pp. 104–8.

7. Letter to Leonard Moore, quoted in Hammond, *Orwell Companion* p. 162.

8. Letter to Orwell quoted in Crick, *George Orwell: A Life*, p. 340. Empson's study of the essential plurality of meaning in literature is *Seven Types of Ambiguity* (London: Chatto & Windus, 1930).

9. G. Woodcock, *The Crystal Spirit* (London: Jonathan Cape, 1967) p. 156.

10. W. J. West suggests that the simple style and conciseness of *Animal Farm*, as well as the speed at which it was written, owe much to the work that Orwell was doing towards the end of his period at the BBC, namely, the adaptation of stories for broadcast. Clearly a concise and clear product was required; and Orwell apparently worked on these adaptations at great speed, under much pressure from administrative business, often having only one day to rewrite a story. One of the texts he adapted was Ignazio Silone's *The Fox*, according to West 'a political allegory set in a pig farm'. See W. J. West, *Orwell: The War Broadcasts* (London: Duckworth, 1985) pp. 60–61, and *The Larger Evils* (Edinburgh: Canongate Press, 1992) pp. 64–5.

11. Hammond, *Orwell Companion*, p. 164.

12. On 'we' and consensus in public discourse, see R. Fowler, *Language in the News* (London: Routledge, 1991); J. Hartley, *Understanding News* (London: Methuen, 1982).

13. On speech acts, see J. R. Searle, *Speech Acts* (Cambridge: Cambridge University Press, 1969); S. C. Levinson, *Pragmatics* (Cambridge: Cambridge University Press, 1983).

ROBERT PEARCE

Orwell, Tolstoy, and Animal Farm

Leo Tolstoy and George Orwell are sometimes contrasted as two figures
with totally opposite attitudes to life, the one an other-worldly believer and
the other a this-worldly humanist. In a celebrated essay, published in 1947,[1]
Orwell defended Shakespeare's *King Lear* against the Russian's intemperate
attack and, moreover, also criticized his whole outlook on life. Tolstoy, he
wrote, was an imperious and egotistical bully, and he quoted his biographer
Derrick Leon that he would frequently 'slap the faces of those with whom
he disagreed'.[2] Orwell wrote that Tolstoy was incapable of either tolerance or
humility; and he considered that his attack on the artistic integrity of *Lear*
arose partly because it was too near the knuckle. Lear's 'huge and gratuitous
act of renunciation' bore an uncomfortably close resemblance to Tolstoy's
similarly foolish renunciation in old age of worldly wealth, sexuality, and
other ties that bind us to 'the surface of the earth—including love, in the
ordinary sense of caring more for one human being than another'.[3] But this,
according to Orwell, was what love was all about, and he characterized Tolstoy—and other would-be saints like Gandhi—as forbiddingly inhuman in
their attitudes.[4] He himself cared strongly about 'the surface of the earth'
and was with Shakespeare in his interest in the 'actual process of life'. The
main aim of the puritanical Tolstoy, Orwell believed, was 'to narrow the
range of human consciousness',[5] a process which he himself, in *Nineteen*

From *The Review of English Studies*, New Series, 49, no. 193 (February 1998): 64–69. © 1998
by Oxford University Press.

Eighty-Four and other later writings, was struggling valiantly to counteract. It is very easy therefore to see the two men as polar opposites, in both their temperament and their artistic aims.

Yet this view is quite mistaken. Orwell's criticisms have sometimes been misunderstood; Orwell and Tolstoy had far more in common than is generally realized; and indeed the Russian influenced this peculiarly English writer in several important ways, not least in that—almost certainly—he furnished him with material for one of the most significant episodes in *Animal Farm*. The parallels between this book and Russian history are well known, but the debt owed to Tolstoy's *What I Believe* has never been acknowledged.

In his biography of Tolstoy, A. N. Wilson praises Orwell's image of Tolstoy-as-Lear but insists that this unforgettable depiction of 'the reason' for the attack on *Lear* is misleading because it distracts our attention from Tolstoy's more deep-seated motivation, which Wilson sees as an 'unconscious envy'.[6] But this is a misreading of Orwell's essay. The likeness between Tolstoy and Lear was, according to Orwell, only one reason for the diatribe against Shakespeare; and towards the end of his essay he pointed to another source of inspiration, the rivalry which the great Russian novelist felt towards perhaps his only rival in world literature.[7] Elsewhere, Orwell referred directly to Tolstoy's jealousy of Shakespeare.[8] Wilson has therefore stolen Orwell's clothes. Indeed too often Orwell's views on Tolstoy have been treated superficially. In fact he felt tremendous admiration for Tolstoy, and his 1947 attack was unrestrained only because he had found an 'opponent' worthy of his mettle. Hence it was, in many ways, a sign of respect. In a broadcast in 1941, he insisted that if 'so great a man as Tolstoy' could not destroy Shakespeare's reputation, then surely no one else could.[9]

Orwell read *War and Peace* several times, first when he was about 20. His sole quarrel with the book, despite its three stout volumes, was that it did not go on long enough. Its characters, he later recalled, 'were people about whom one would gladly go on reading for ever'.[10] He judged that Tolstoy's creations had international appeal and that therefore one could hold imaginary conversations with figures like Pierre Bezukhov. Such men and women seemed to be engaged in the process of making their souls, and therefore Tolstoy's grasp was 'so much larger than Dickens's'.[11] This was high praise indeed, and even when criticizing Tolstoy's attack on Shakespeare he paid a passing tribute to *War and Peace* and *Anna Karenina*.[12] Nor was Orwell familiar only with these classics. He also read *The Cossacks, Sebastopol*, and other works, including the later short stories, written with parable-like simplicity. Indeed, such was his regard for Tolstoy that he went to considerable trouble to read several of his more obscure works. He even judged that Tolstoy would still be a remarkable man if he had written nothing except his polemical pamphlets, for no one could read him and still feel quite the same about life.[13]

There is no evidence that Orwell read all of Tolstoy's translated writings. We do not know, for instance, whether he read a compendium of Tolstoy's religious writings translated by Aylmer Maude and published by Oxford University Press in 1940 as *A Confession: The Gospel in Brief and What I Believe*. Certainly there was no copy among Orwell's books at his death. Yet this is the book which, I wish to argue, influenced *Animal Farm*. It may be that Orwell came to it second-hand, by the extracts quoted in Derrick Leon's biography of Tolstoy, which Orwell read on publication early in 1944, referred to in his 'As I Please' column in *Tribune* and reviewed for the *Observer*, describing it as 'an outstanding book'.[14] He was reading it just as he was working hard to complete *Animal Farm*.

Everyone is familiar with the parallels between Russian history and the plot of *Animal Farm*. Perhaps indeed we are over-familiar with them, for the details of the book had a wider totalitarian relevance than to any one country, and Orwell borrowed from Italian history ('Mussolini is always right') and from German, as well as from Russian. But there is one issue in the book for which there seems no real-life equivalent: this is the rewriting of the original revolutionary aims, the principles of Animalism. Admittedly revolutionary idealism in Russia and elsewhere was betrayed and perverted, but there was no outward repudiation of Marxist rhetoric. Although Stalin ignored such theory in his actions and imposed his will by force of arms and propaganda, he never ceased to pay lip-service to the original ideals. Even when he was arraigning the Old Bolsheviks in the Show Trials of the 1930s, he was at pains to assert that it was they—not he—who had sinned against the holy writ of Marxist-Leninist ideology. So what inspired Orwell's brilliant and hard-hitting reformulations?

First, we must look at the precise ways in which the Commandments of the first chapter of *Animal Farm* were perverted in the course of the book. 'No animal shall sleep in a bed' became 'No animal shall sleep in a bed *with sheets*'. 'No animal shall drink alcohol' changed into 'No animal shall drink alcohol *to excess*'. 'No animal shall kill any other animal' became 'No animal shall kill another animal *without cause*'. Most famously of all, 'All animals are equal' became 'All animals are equal but some animals are more equal than others'. In short, each commandment received a coda, a reservation which effectively reversed its meaning.

There is no parallel to this in Russian political history. But Leo Tolstoy had observed a very similar perversion, in Russian religious history, as Leon recounts in his biography. What Tolstoy considered the essential precepts of the Sermon on the Mount had become almost their opposites in the mouths of Russian Orthodox clerics. The original 'Do not be angry' had become 'Do not be angry *without a cause*'.[15] The phrase 'without a cause' was, to Tolstoy, the key to an understanding of the perversion of scripture. Of course everyone who is angry justifies himself with a cause, however trivial or unjust, and therefore he guessed, correctly as he soon found, that the words were a later interpolation designed to devalue the original injunction. Similarly the instructions not to promise anything on oath, not to resist evil by violence, and not to judge or go to law had all been overturned, and had become their opposites, when the church had sought accommodation with the civil power.

Orwell's reading of the extracts from Tolstoy in Leon's biography, as detailed above, may well have inspired his rewriting of the principles of Animalism. This, of course, is not to denigrate Orwell's achievement. It was he who had, first, to see the appositeness to his own work of the banal—but contextually brilliant—'without a cause' and, then, to invent similar reservations. But it is to insist that the provenance of the details of *Animal Farm* is far wider than the painful period of history through which Orwell lived. It is also to contend that Tolstoy was an important influence on Orwell.

Although this may be considered more speculative, it is quite possible that Orwell actually read the original Tolstoy, either before Leon's book was published or as a result of seeing its brief extracts. We do know that Orwell was prepared to search 'all over London' to track down a Tolstoyan quarry;[16] and as a bibliophile he was always well aware of new material being published, even in the dark days of 1940. The fact that, for effect, Orwell italicized his codas as did Tolstoy, though Leon's quotations were all in roman script,[17] is added evidence for this. If he did consult the original translation by Aylmer Maude, Orwell would have found other neat reformulations by Tolstoy which may well have influenced his own. To say 'do not be angry *without a cause*', Tolstoy decided, was like urging someone to 'Love the neighbour whom thou approvest of'.[18] He also drew attention to the 1864 edition of the Catechism which, after quoting each of the Ten Commandments, then gave 'a reservation which cancelled it'. For instance, the commandment to honour one God had an addendum to the effect that we should also honour the angels and saints, 'besides, of course, the Mother of God and the three persons of the Trinity'. The second commandment, not to make idols, was perverted into an injunction to make obeisance before icons; the third, not to take oaths, became a demand to swear when called upon to do so by the legal authorities. The command to honour one's mother and father degenerated into a call to honour also the Tsar, the ministers of the church, and all those in authority—specified on three long pages! 'Thou shalt not kill' was interpreted ingeniously. One should not kill 'except in the fulfilment of one's duties'.[19]

The similarity between the methods employed in the relevant passages of Tolstoy and Orwell is astonishing. The most obvious way of accounting for this is by direct influence. There are indeed other indications that Orwell's reading and rereading of Tolstoy left its mark on his work. May not the character of Boxer in *Animal Farm* have been influenced by the long-suffering talking horse who was carried off to the knacker at the end of Tolstoy's short story 'Strider: The Story of a Horse'? Orwell's concept of Doublethink may also have owed something to a superb example from Vronsky's code of principles, in *Anna Karenina*, 'that one must pay a cardsharper, but need not pay a tailor; that one must never tell a lie to a man, but one may to a woman; *that one must never cheat anyone, but one may a husband;* that one must never pardon an insult, but may give one, and so on'. The arresting opening of *Homage to Catalonia* may also owe a debt to Tolstoy. Orwell took an 'immediate liking' to an unnamed, tough-looking Italian, whose face somehow deeply moved him. This episode, whose authenticity historians must doubt, bears a close resemblance to the passage in *War and Peace* where Pierre and Davôut gaze at each other and, in so doing, see each other's essential humanity. Similarly the execution, in the same book, contains details resembling those Orwell included in 'A Hanging'. Orwell's Burmese prisoner steps aside to avoid a puddle, despite the fact that he will soon be dead. In the same way, Tolstoy's Russian prisoner adjusts the uncomfortable knot of his blindfold just before the execution squad put an end to his life. Finally, Tolstoy is undoubtedly relevant to the nightmare world of *Nineteen Eighty-Four*. The Russian wondered when the priests would understand 'that even in the face of death, two and two still make four';[20] Orwell knew that some priests would never admit any such thing and that, after Room 101, even Winston Smith might accept that '2 + 2 = 5'.[21]

Of course it may be merely a coincidence—or a series of coincidences—that Orwell's rewriting of the Seven Commandments bears such a strong resemblance to Tolstoy's exposure of the perversion of the Ten Commandments, and that there are, in addition, other parallels in their writings which seem best explained by direct, if perhaps unconscious, influence. But if so, then this is good evidence that the two men had far more in common than anyone has ever pointed out. Certainly their self-presentations were similar. Tolstoy once called himself 'a quite enfeebled, good-for-nothing parasite, who can only exist under the most exceptional conditions found only when thousands of people labour to support a life that is of no value to anyone'.[22] Orwell did not go quite as far as that; but he was the British equivalent. 'I am a degenerate modern semi-intellectual who would die if I did not get my early morning cup of tea and my *New Statesman* every Friday.'[23] On the surface, the two men seem so different, but the fact is that there were many similarities between them.[24] (Who realizes, without looking up the dates, that their deaths were separated by only forty years?) Orwell may have castigated Tolstoy as otherworldly, but both men seemed essentially puritanical to others. Whereas the one insisted on making his own shoes, the other would try to make his own furniture, and both went to considerable pains to grow their own food. Each was an enemy of the machine age. Both were dedicated writers, both moralists and humanitarians, and both polemicists. After writing discursive books early in their careers, each of them was an 'engaged' writer later in life. They needed a mission, or purpose, in life and shared the opinion that man could not live by hedonism alone. In addition, they berated mere intellectuals. Neither would passively accept what he was told: each had to work ideas out for himself, displaying great intellectual self-confidence—and considerable unorthodoxy—in the process. Should we compare them as religious thinkers? Certainly there are religious aspects to Orwell's thought.[25] Should we, as George Woodcock argues, even compare Orwell's repudiation of his education and his quitting of his career in the imperial civil service with Tolstoy's renunciations,[26] or his migration to Jura with Tolstoy's flight from Yasnaya Polyana to Astapovo? If so, then Orwell's criticisms of Tolstoy in 1947 were similar to Tolstoy's of Shakespeare in 1906, in that both were motivated by 'a half-recognized similarity'.[27] Obviously such comparisons may be pushed too far. What does seem clear, however, is that the connections between these two figures are worth recognizing, and also worth further study.

Notes

1. *The Collected Essays, Journalism and Letters of George Orwell* (hereafter *CEJL*) (Harmondsworth, 1970), iv. 331–48: 'Lear, Tolstoy and the Fool'.

2. Ibid. 339.

3. Ibid. 339, 344.

4. Ibid. 527.

5. Ibid. 338; ibid. i. 28.

6. A. N. Wilson, *Tolstoy* (London, 1988), 480.

7. *CEJL* iv. 347: 'The more pleasure people took in Shakespeare, the less they would listen to Tolstoy.'

8. Ibid, ii. 154.

9. Ibid. 157.

10. Ibid. iii. 129.

11. Ibid. i. 500.

12. Ibid. iv. 348.

13. *CEJL* ii. 156, 223; *Observer*, 26 Mar. 1944.

14. Ibid. iii. 129; *Observer*, 26 Mar. 1944: I am grateful to Professor Peter Davison for providing me with a photocopy of Orwell's review.

15. D. Leon, *Tolstoy: His Life and Work* (London, 1944), 200.

16. *CEJL* ii. 156.

17. Leon, *Tolstoy*, 199–200; Leo Tolstoy, *A Confession: The Gospel in Brief and What I Believe* (Oxford, 1940), 372.

18. Tolstoy, *Confession*, 373.

19. Tolstoy, *Confession*, 496–7.

20. For these and other parallels, see my editions of *The Sayings of George Orwell* (London, 1994) and *The Sayings of Leo Tolstoy* (London, 1995).

21. P. Davison, *George Orwell, A Literary Life* (London, 1996), 134.

22. Leo Tolstoy, *What Then Must We Do?*, trans. A. Maude (Oxford, 1935), p. xvi.

23. George Orwell, *The Road to Wigan Pier* (Harmondsworth, 1962), 184.

24. R. Rees, *George Orwell: Fugitive from the Camp of Victory* (London, 1961), 114: 'It seems to me that Orwell was a good deal nearer to the other-worldly Tolstoy and Gandhi and a good deal further from the average humanistic progressive than he himself was prepared to recognise.'

25. For interesting comments on this issue, see S. Ingle, *George Orwell: A Political Life* (Manchester, 1993), 21–35, 108–11.

26. G. Woodcock, *The Crystal Spirit* (London, 1967), 242.

27. Ibid.

ANTHONY STEWART

An Absence of Pampering: The Betrayal of the Rebellion and the End of Decency in Animal Farm

Between the pigs and human beings there was not, and there need not be, any clash of interests whatever. Their struggles and their difficulties were one. Was not the labour problem the same everywhere? Here it became apparent that Mr. Pilkington was about to spring some carefully prepared witticism on the company, but for a moment he was too overcome by amusement to be able to utter it. After much choking, during which his various chins turned purple, he managed to get it out: 'If you have your lower animals to contend with,' he said, 'we have our lower classes!' This bon mot set the table in a roar; and Mr. Pilkington once again congratulated the pigs on the low rations, the long working hours, and the general absence of pampering which he had observed on Animal Farm.

—Orwell, *Animal Farm*

From 1935 to *Nineteen Eighty-Four:*
Concerns for the Part Become Concerns for the Whole

. . . [W]hen examined based on the doubleness of their perspectives and their ability to treat others decently, both John Flory and Gordon Comstock reveal character flaws that subject them to the negative evaluation of the narrators of their stories, negative evaluations which the narrators encourage the reader to share. The two protagonists' shortcomings stand out in full relief when they are seen in contrast to the figures in the novels

From *George Orwell, Doubleness, and the Value of Decency*, pp. 93–122, 174–79. © 2003 by Taylor & Francis Books, published by Routledge.

who do see themselves in relation to others and are therefore able to behave decently towards those around them. Flory is duplicitous; he attempts to win Elizabeth's affections by impressing her with his expertise regarding Burmese culture. He attempts to appear knowledgeable about and sympathetic to the Burmese but is so self-absorbed that he cannot see that such sympathy actually offends the bigoted Elizabeth. But what masquerades as sympathy is exposed as selfishness and condescension through Flory's relationships with Ma Hla May and Veraswami, respectively. By the end of the novel he appears to have received what he deserves when his duplicity is finally exposed for all to see in the church, the scene that finally convinces him of his complete lack of place within the compartmentalized social world of *Burmese Days*, a recognition that results in his suicide.

Gordon Comstock's pronouncements against the "money-god" are ultimately also revealed as hollow. Whereas Flory is duplicitous, Gordon is petty and childish. When he actually receives some money, he behaves in a manner completely out of keeping with the anticapitalist declarations he has been clinging to since he was sixteen years of age and which he has not seen fit to rethink since. His obnoxiousness towards Ravelston and Rosemary, as well as his selfishness in not giving any of the money he received for publishing a poem to his long-suffering sister, Julia, are especially unpleasant when compared to the decency and integrity shown by Rosemary and even the well-meaning, although overly accommodating, Ravelston. When Gordon is told that Rosemary is pregnant, he is—more than anything else—relieved that he need not continue his political charade any longer and may finally enter middle-class adulthood.

Flory is a white Englishman trying (when he has the pluck, as he says to Elizabeth) to resist the demands of colonialist orthodoxy while living in an imperial outpost. Gordon is a member of the middle-middle class who has literary ambitions but lacks the Oxbridge imprimatur he sees as necessary for acceptance in the world of the highbrow literary salon. Their respective vulnerabilities (Flory's birthmark, Gordon's relative poverty) would initially suggest that each could benefit greatly from seeing himself and his interests in relation to others and contributing a more doubled perspective to the stratified world in which he finds himself, instead of reflexively putting his own needs ahead of others'. The fostering of such a perspective might have enabled each man to express a more nuanced point of view rather than merely railing self-piteously against what he sees as the injustices that befall only him. However, each shows an unflattering willingness to accept the social and political rules he ostensibly criticizes when those rules play to his advantage. Gordon's growth at the end of *Aspidistra* is only made possible once he steps outside of his own childish concerns—sees through a glass, darkly—and begins to imagine what Rosemary is going through with her pregnancy and the development of their unborn child.

Burmese Days and *Keep the Aspidistra Flying* have not worn particularly well as time has passed since their first publications. Both seem, in the early twenty-first century, dated period pieces, interesting as attempts to dramatize social and political problems from a specific time, but clearly artifacts from another age. The consequences of the personal failings of Flory and Gordon are relatively minor in the context of the larger worlds depicted in the novels. Even though Flory commits suicide, his is just the act of one desperate man. The society which leads him to his self-destruction continues on largely as it always has, as evidenced by the epilogue which concludes *Burmese Days*, in which, among other things, Elizabeth marries Macgregor and "fills with complete success the position for which Nature had designed her from the first, that of a *burra* memsahib" (300). It's like Flory never existed in Kyauktada at all. Similarly, Gordon returns to the "good" job he previously scorned and marries his sweetheart. His lofty preachings against the money-god might as well have never been uttered as he is absorbed into the adult mainstream, as so many adolescent rebels who bemoan this "measly manner of existence" (in Biff Loman's memorable phrase) eventually are. Neither man exercises any influence over the society in which he lives. In fact, the societies operate largely oblivious to the machinations of these two interesting but socially insignificant men.

Reading *Burmese Days* and *Keep the Aspidistra Flying* through a lens focused on the value of decency places them in a context that enables a clear connection with the two famous novels that stand principally as Orwell's legacy. This context suggests for these two earlier books an updated relevance to our much more diverse and changing world. It also provides valuable insight into the priorities that underlie Orwell's version of socialism and leads logically to an examination of *Animal Farm* and *Nineteen Eighty-Four*. As already mentioned, Flory and Gordon occupy positions of vulnerability which might otherwise have inspired them to make more constructive contributions than they do within the worlds in which they live. More importantly, though, such a constructive contribution is possible for any individual and is not the exclusive preserve of an elite. At bottom, the importance of decency lies in its potentially beneficial effect on the larger society.

Similarly, Orwell's socialism concentrates less on the theory—which he found accomplished very little in the world of the everyday, except to alienate those who might benefit most from socialism—and more on practice that could be enacted by anyone.[1] "Socialism, as now presented," he writes in *The Road to Wigan Pier*, "is unattractive largely because it appears, at any rate from the outside, to be the plaything of cranks, doctrinaires, parlour Bolsheviks and so forth. But it is worth remembering that this is only so because the cranks, doctrinaires, etc., have been allowed to get there first; if the movement were invaded by better brains and more common decency, the objectionable types would cease to dominate it" (204–05). This nontheoretical version of socialism is predicated upon the influence of better brains (by which he means people more concerned with the best potential outcomes of socialism and not merely doctrine or theory) and upon the common decency that enables a more inclusive discussion of socialism (including more engagement with and respect for the considerations of those who are usually excluded from the conversation but whose input would probably benefit socialism as a whole). Decency promises a victory of democracy over elitism.

In his attempt to convince both his socialist readers (that they must think about socialism in ways that are more inclusive) and his nonsocialist readers (that socialism is worthy of a sympathetic hearing), he emphasizes the benefits available to both groups. Using a characteristically simple and vivid image to encapsulate his point, he writes in *Wigan Pier*: "We have got to fight for justice and liberty, and Socialism does mean justice and liberty when the nonsense is stripped off it. It is only the essentials that are worth remembering. To recoil from Socialism because so many individual Socialists are inferior people is as absurd as refusing to travel by train because you dislike the ticket-collector's face" (205). *Wigan Pier* emphasizes the importance of a common interest between the various potential adherents to socialism: "All that is needed is to hammer two facts home into the public consciousness. One, that the interest of all exploited people are the same; the other, that Socialism is compatible with common decency" (214). His concern with how socialism is perceived in the public consciousness makes plain Orwell's ongoing priority: the benefits of socialism reside in making as broad as possible the base of potential followers and that the people who embrace socialism need only accept the importance of treating others decently in order for it to become a viable political and social framework. This priority is something anyone can understand, irrespective of his or her level of theoretical knowledge of socialism in particular or formal education in general. The implicit judgments made about Flory and Gordon in their narratives suggest that nothing except their own duplicity and childishness, respectively, stops these two men from behaving better than they do. The presence of their admirable, socially subordinate companions only emphasizes this point further.

* * *

What has yet to be examined in this study of the role of the tandem values of doubleness and decency in Orwell's fiction is the case that preoccupies the writer from about 1936, and his involvement in the Spanish Civil War, until the end of his life. This is the case in which the emergence of a totalitarian regime outlaws entirely the doubled perspective and therefore renders decency impossible. In *Burmese Days* and *Keep the Aspidistra Flying*, the protagonists do not choose to act decently towards others because their own selfish motives negate their ability to adopt a doubled sensibility. While the two men may be criticized for their lack of decency, their failings do not prohibit others from behaving in a more admirable manner, hence the importance once again of contrasting figures like Veraswami, Rosemary, and, in a different way, Ravelston. But each of Orwell's last two novels presents a powerful class that is able to impose its own narrow, exclusive point of view on those under its power. In these novels, when decency emerges, it does not become just an incidental part of the landscape; it is an aberration that the ruling class feels must be stamped out. Orwell's fear of totalitarianism manifests itself in two nightmare visions in which the individual's relationship with the world around him or her must coincide exactly with the point of view of the ruling class. Such a state of affairs makes it impossible for one to hold a doubled perspective; only one point of view is acceptable.

In "Why I Write," Orwell declares: "Every line of serious work that I have written since 1936 has been written, directly or indirectly, *against* totalitarianism and *for* democratic Socialism, as I understand it. It seems to me nonsense, in a period like our own, to think that one can avoid writing of such things" (18.319). "Writers and Leviathan," written two years after "Why I Write," makes a similar point about how the times in which the writer lived dictated his subject matter: "This is a political age. War, Fascism, concentration camps, rubber truncheons, atomic bombs, etc., are what we daily think about, and therefore to a great extent what we write about, even when we do not name them openly. We cannot help this. When you are on a sinking ship, your thoughts will be about sinking ships" (19.288). Ian Slater points out how this preoccupation with the pressing issues of the day expresses itself in Orwell's earlier and later fiction:

> Before [Orwell's] Spanish experience, in such books as *Keep the Aspidistra Flying*, he saw the basis of moral relativism as being mainly one of money, reflecting the rich-versus-poor view of Eric Blair. After Spain, the basis of moral relativism in his work shifts from money to power. Whereas Gordon Comstock angrily declares that God is money, Winston Smith despairingly concedes that 'GOD IS POWER.' (165–66)[2]

The political age of which Orwell speaks in "Writers and Leviathan" inspires the form that finally enables him to address the issues of the day on a scale that comprehends more than the inner conflicts of mere individuals. In the last two novels he moves to representing the broader social and political implications of the emergence of powerful and ruthless classes as opposed to merely self-interested individuals.

As we turn in this and the next chapter to the most famous of Orwell's books, it is crucial to recognize that both present artificial societies of the author's making. Not only do these societies operate despite the criticisms of their individual citizens, as was the case in *Burmese Days* and *Keep the Aspidistra Flying*, they actively dictate the behavior of their citizens and severely punish even the slightest divergence from the extremely narrow precepts they set out. As Orwell turns his fiction to the implications of this kind of total power, he continues to work out the question that is so important to him, the question he articulates late in his life: "Can we get men to behave decently to each other if they no longer believe in God?" (Meyers 294). The affirmative answer to this question is contained in the simple values of "justice and common decency" (*Wigan Pier* 164), which are, for him, the revolutionary potential of socialism at its best.

Animal Farm and *Nineteen Eighty-Four*, at first glance, appear to answer this pressing question in the negative. The oppression of the animals by Napoleon and of the citizens of Oceania by the Inner Party are both predicated upon uncompromisingly narrow points of view rendering a sense of decency dangerous to the self as well as practically impossible. But as is always the case with Orwell, the answer to the question is more mixed, more doubled, than the simple negative. While it is true that the citizens within these societies lack freedom and are treated in ways that are anything but decent, the optimistic fact remains that decent individuals still emerge even from under such repression. In both books, the conflict between the indecent regime and the decent individual may be read as a conflict between the regime's desire to prohibit its citizens' ability to view the world through a doubled perspective and a willingness on the part of at least some of the citizens to risk their lives if necessary in order to preserve this crucial freedom to see their place in the world in more complex terms than is officially sanctioned by the powerful.

In what remains of this chapter I will examine *Animal Farm*, in which the significance of decency may be seen quite clearly through an examination of the three most important developments in the novella: the animals' rebellion, the incremental consolidation of Napoleon's power, and the death of Boxer. Approaching Orwell's "fairy story," as he ironically subtitles it, through these three developments enables a discussion of an aspect of decency that I have not yet undertaken—the risks of behaving in this fashion, especially when powerful forces insist that the world and relationships between individuals be viewed in the way they prescribe and only in this way.

Animal Farm points up the fact that championing the value of decency may actually come at the cost of one's own life, as is the case with Boxer. Nevertheless, Boxer is the most admirable of the animals and his admirable nature may be traced in large measure to his willingness to see himself and his interests in relation to those of others instead of narrowly and selfishly. But this same willingness that casts Boxer as an admirable figure ends up making him a useful instrument to the oppressive Napoleon. In contrast to Boxer, Napoleon exhibits a narrow, monomaniacal perspective that he enforces ruthlessly and to which all the animals must submit in order to preserve their own lives. In addition to the emergence of a decent character within this indecent environment, *Animal Farm* ends on a note that suggests the pigs' power over the farm is hardly absolute and will eventually come to an end. Including this suggestion within the novella instead of a conclusion in which the pigs are simply victorious over the other animals, provides another view of what might be called Orwell's mitigated optimism, his "pessimism of the intellect and optimism of the will," to borrow an expression used to describe Antonio Gramsci and which also typifies Orwell.

The Rebellion—The Beginning of the End of Decency

The first two novels required some plot synopsis by way of introduction because of their relative obscurity today. However, the story of the animals who take over their owner's farm but whose rebellion is then betrayed by the pigs' usurpation of power, headed by an autocratic pig named Napoleon, is well known to just about anyone who completed secondary school in an English-speaking country, and it need not be rehearsed again here.[3] "In its general effect," as Richard Smyer writes, in accounting for the fable's sustained popularity, "Orwell's style of writing in *Animal Farm* is nonhierarchical and egalitarian. And despite its simplicity, the language is flexible enough to convey a range of conditions and attitudes—from the unadorned descriptions of Clover's solicitude to the intellectual abstractness of Snowball's Latinate vocabulary, from the pathetic earnestness of Boxer's uplift slogans to Squealer's molasses-smooth sophistries" (8). Leaving aside the specifics of the historical allegory, *Animal Farm* may be read more broadly as another expression of the complexities contained within the ostensibly simple value of decency. This reading presents a variation of the question: 'can human beings behave decently towards one another when they no longer believe in God.' The variation is, 'what is the price of decency and is this price worth paying when one is confronted by an individual or class for whom decency is not valuable at all and who holds enough power to impose this attitude on others?'

Old Major, the "prize Middle White boar" (1) and patriarch of the animals on the farm, tells the other animals what he sees as the true nature of an animal's life ("miserable, laborious, and short" [3]). His main purpose in the narrative is to prophesy that at some point in time, "it might be in a week or in a hundred years" (5), animals will rebel against the injustices inflicted upon them by their human masters. He also warns the others that they must not repeat the evil ways of humanity:

> And remember also that in fighting against Man, we must not come to resemble him. Even when you have conquered him, do not adopt his vices. No animals must ever live in a house, or sleep in a bed, or wear clothes, or drink alcohol, or smoke tobacco, or touch money, or engage in trade. All the habits of Man are evil. And above all, no animals must ever tyrannize over his own kind. Weak or strong, clever or simple, we are all brothers. No animal must ever kill any other animal. All animals are equal. (6)

Major lays out the basic tenets of what the pigs eventually codify as "Animalism," the seven commandments of which they write on the wall of a barn. Clearly, Major's warnings are based on the simple notion of decency, that each animal, weak or strong, clever or simple, must be aware of itself in relation to the others on the farm. Animalism is based on the view of the human being as a worthless parasite, "the only creature that consumes without producing" (4), and one that is incapable of taking into account the best interest of its fellow human beings, let alone the concerns of animals. Instead, humans feed animals only enough to keep them alive while they are useful and then they are slaughtered, drowned, or sent to the knacker once they have been exhausted by their enemies' demands.

Major's lecture to the other animals announces clearly the difference between *Animal Farm* and *Nineteen Eighty-Four* and the two novels already examined here. His unequivocal excoriation of humanity would at first appear to argue against the notion of decency at the heart of his teachings. After all, he is uncompromising in his hatred of humanity's ways and leaves no room for the prospect of a "good" human being. But he is actually pointing out that there are injustices in the world which he has seen over his twelve years of life, knowledge which he feels he must pass on to the younger animals before he dies. His account of the harsh realities that exist in the relationship between animals and human beings includes the following dire warning:

> And remember, comrades, your resolution must never falter. No argument must lead you astray. Never listen when they tell you that Man and the animals have a common interest, that the prosperity of the one is the prosperity of the others. It is all lies. Man serves

the interests of no creature except himself. And among us animals let there be perfect unity, perfect comradeship in the struggle. All men are enemies. All animals are comrades. (5–6)

Major's caution against arguments contradicting his account of humanity's selfishness is crucial in its foreshadowing of the betrayal of the rebellion which is to follow. He introduces here the importance of propaganda, which sets the interests of some against those of others, and which Napoleon will use expertly to keep the other animals in line as he consolidates his own power. Major's warnings to let no "argument" lead them astray, and not to listen when "they" say that human beings and animals share a common interest, point up the fact that the animals will face those who will attempt to convince them of things that are not true in order to push an agenda on them that is not in their best interest. This is an important detail for Orwell to include in the novella because it makes the point that the innocent decency of Major's version of Animalism (and possibly Orwell's own version of socialism) may not in fact be equipped for the real world of politics, where might may indeed make right and the values of decency may simply be overwhelmed in the face of an unscrupulous and powerful foe.

After the animals drive Jones from the farm, the pigs immediately take the leadership role. The most prominent pigs—Napoleon, Snowball, and Squealer—quickly emerge as first among ostensible equals: "Napoleon was a large, rather fierce-looking Berkshire boar, the only Berkshire on the farm, not much of a talker but with a reputation for getting his own way. Snowball was a more vivacious pig than Napoleon, quicker in speech and more inventive, but was not considered to have the same depth of character" (9). Squealer, "a small fat pig . . . with very round cheeks, twinkling eyes, nimble movements, and a shrill voice" (9) is a "brilliant talker" (9) who the others say "could turn black into white" (9) with his words. These descriptions hint at the important role speech and the ability to manipulate words will play in the story. Snowball's vivacious quickness in speech and his inventiveness suggest a leader who might be able to conceive a forward-thinking plan like a windmill, as he does. Squealer's ability to turn black into white marks him as a valuable underling when Napoleon finally seizes power for himself. In addition, Squealer is a porker—a pig to be fattened for meat, as are most of the pigs when Jones owns the farm—rather than a boar to be bred up for sale, as are Napoleon and Snowball. Squealer, then, is bred to be subordinate to the other two no matter which ultimately emerges as the farm's leader.

The first description of Napoleon also draws our attention, for the moment, back to the details of the allegory, as he is the only Berkshire boar on the farm. This detail suggests that he is not related to Major, even though

Major has fathered "over four hundred children" (5) during his time on Manor Farm. Napoleon's lineage as a Berkshire, then, puts him in the minority, as was Stalin, after whom Napoleon is modeled. Stalin was Georgian and as such a member of an ethnic minority within the Soviet power structure. The significance of lineage is revisited later in the tale when the four sows on the farm all litter simultaneously and all the piglets are piebald: "as Napoleon was the only boar on the farm, it was possible to guess at their parentage" (75). So Napoleon's cult of personality effects the beginning of a change in the make-up of the pigs' population, in which his breed increases from a minority of one to a more prominent position in terms of numbers and, more importantly, power. This shift in the predominant breed of the pigs is just one of the many ways in which it is made clear that Napoleon's is not a nature that is likely to accede to the interests of others but one that will make others submit to him. The introductory description, as was the case in the earlier novels, imparts a great deal of important information in a small space. Napoleon's interests will be his alone and considerations of his position in relation to that of others will play no part in his politics. He is able to turn what might have been a weakness—his minority position—into a strength, at the cost of almost everyone else on the farm.

* * *

In the immediate aftermath of the rebellion, Napoleon is not alone in recognizing the pigs' opportunity to become a privileged class. While the history upon which the novella is based demands that some group emerge to lead the animals, it is crucial that the pigs immediately separate themselves from—and place themselves above—the other animals by identifying themselves as intellectuals.[4] They teach themselves to read and write—in secret: "The pigs now revealed that during the past three months they had taught themselves to read and write from an old spelling book which had belonged to Mr. Jones's children and which had been thrown on the rubbish heap" (15).[5] That they establish this superiority in secret and then display it to the other animals demonstrates that all of the pigs, including Snowball, are willing to press the advantage of their cleverness on the others. Subsequently, the pigs teach the others to read and write, and eventually "almost every animal on the farm was literate in some degree" (20), but the class division is already firmly in place. As the animals learn and begin to sing "Beasts of England"—the anthem of the rebellion—the division is made even more explicit: "Even the stupidest of them had already picked up the tune and a few of the words, and as for the clever ones, such as the pigs and dogs, they had the entire song by heart within a few minutes" (8). The superiority of the pigs, and the eventual role of the dogs as Napoleon's private police force, is established based on a hierarchy of "cleverness."

That the ruling class on the postrebellion farm is a group of intellectuals that emerges from within the rank and file of the animals makes *Animal Farm* look at first like an instance of what Antonio Gramsci called the "organic intellectual," the group of leaders that arises, according to him, simultaneously within any new class's development. Organic intellectuals "are for the most part 'specialisations' of partial aspects of the primitive activity of the new social type which the new class has brought into prominence" (6). In other words, they represent a partial expression of the new class, but are presumed to share the interests of the new class as a whole. This type of intellectual envisaged by Gramsci is responsible for

> active participation in practical life, as constructor, organiser, 'permanent persuader' and not just a simple orator (but superior at the same time to the abstract mathematical spirit); from technique-as-work one proceeds to technique-as-science and to the humanistic conception of history, without which one remains 'specialised' and does not become 'directive' (specialised and political). (10)

Gramsci's theory does not envisage an elitist class of intellectuals but a group whose activity is completely integrated into the interests and desires of the other members of the class. "Since its inception," as Carl Boggs explains,

> Marxism has always presented itself as a transformative theory and practice, whatever the geopolitical setting. As the most powerful framework of the twentieth century, it inspired the development of three main types of intellectuals: Jacobin (elite intervention), critical (radical opposition of dispersed individuals or groups), and organic (tied to fundamental social groups and classes). (118)

The former two types suggest a separate, often privileged, elite operating outside the run of "everyday" people. The touchstone expression of these types of intellectual is Julian Benda's conservative classic, *The Betrayal of the Intellectuals*.[6] Gramsci speaks of intellectuals, instead, strictly in terms of their function *within* society and therefore is willing to assert the following:

> When one distinguishes between intellectuals and non-intellectuals, one is referring in reality only to the immediate social function of the professional category of the intellectuals, that is, one has in

mind the direction in which their specific professional activity is weighted, whether towards intellectual elaboration or towards muscular-nervous effort. This means that, although one can speak of intellectuals, one cannot speak of non-intellectuals, because non-intellectuals do not exist. (9)

"All men are intellectuals, one could therefore say," he writes, summarizing the point, "but not all men have in society the function of intellectuals" (9). This is a radical and useful addition to the ongoing antagonism between "intellectuals" and "nonintellectuals," to which Orwell is very sensitive, an antagonism I touched on in my introduction, because it acknowledges the equal worth of those who do not function as intellectuals within society. Gramsci's emphasis on the *function* of different elements within a class or society acknowledges differences without imposing a hierarchy on these different roles.

Conceiving of intellectuals as Gramsci does produces a number of benefits, not the least of which is the sort of doubled awareness that enables those who function as intellectuals to keep in mind their organic connection and shared interest with those who perform other functions which are equally important to the larger population. Anne Showstack Sassoon characterizes this benefit of Gramsci's theory as follows: "Gramsci's continual use of terms like specialization, specialist, division of labor, skill, apprenticeship has the effect of demystifying the intellectual function as he tries to grasp changes in the mode of intellectual work" (143). Showstack Sassoon identifies what she calls a "double function" in Gramsci's language:

> It de-mystifies the process so that academic achievement does not appear as a trick, magic, out of our control, or a 'gift of God.' At the same time it stresses the labour involved for most people. By talking about studying as hard work Gramsci emphasises what it has in common with manual labour as well as authenticating the experience of those who find it difficult. (151)

Making a similar point, Carl Boggs notes that Gramsci observed Marxist theory all too often degenerating "into a jargon for intellectual elites alone. Marxist intellectuals, like their traditional counterparts of earlier times, often sought to preserve whatever power and material advantages they could derive from superior education, knowledge, skills, and cultural sophistication" (56–57). This description of the desire to preserve privilege while ostensibly arguing for social change is reminiscent of Orwell's criticism of middle-class socialists in *The Road to Wigan Pier*.[7]

Orwell shares with Gramsci the desire to demystify and democratize the social functions of the intellectual.[8] Bernard Crick describes Orwell's attitude towards Marxists as expressed in *The Road to Wigan Pier* as a "measured criticism, not outright rejection, the kind of criticism that some modern Marxists, followers of Gramsci for instance, would readily accept, or even claim to be the true young Marx" (*Life* 306). Orwell's depiction of the intellectual that emerges in *Animal Farm* may also be seen as a criticism and not a rejection of intellectuals as such, but specifically as a criticism of the pigs' exploitative behavior and exclusive self-interest at the expense of decency.

With the theory of the organic intellectual in mind, it is worth remembering that as the animals set about getting in the first harvest since the expulsion of Jones, the pigs "did not actually work, but directed and supervised the others" (22). In this manner, the cleverest of the animals seem to function in keeping with Gramsci's ideal. The pigs—in organizing the animals, setting down the principles of Animalism in writing, teaching the other animals to read and write, and establishing as a symbolic objective the importance of getting in the harvest "quicker than Jones and his men could do," as Snowball exhorts the other animals (22)—become "directive," according to Gramsci's terminology. They are "specialized" in their ability to assign, organize, and lead the other animals in getting in the harvest, as well as their study of the science necessary to conceive of the windmill and for the strategy of defense when the men attempt to take back the farm the first time. They are also "political" in articulating the importance of the farm's place in history, the significance of the short-term goal of getting in the harvest faster than Jones and his men ever could do, as well as the farm's long-term objectives, to stand as a social system operating without the interference of human hands and to serve as an example to be followed by other animals on farms throughout England.

But for all the initial promise of the rebellion, *Animal Farm* actually ends up demonstrating the central criticism against the theory of the organic intellectual. What Gramsci's theory does not account for, the main weakness critics frequently bring up against his idea, is the simple question of why anyone, especially one with a superior knowledge base, would not act in a selfish manner, as opposed to the selfless, egalitarian manner Gramsci's theory calls for. As John Patrick Diggins writes, Gramsci "leaves us with no understanding why intellectuals would be motivated" to "help workers grasp history and seize power" (150). The suggestion here is that such empowerment would find the intellectuals working towards their own obsolescence. Diggins summarizes the motivational predicament Gramsci creates as follows:

> The true organic intellectual is he who thinks only those thoughts that are potential actions in the emancipation of the working

class. Here lies the supreme irony. Although Gramsci looked to
intellectuals to bring consciousness and freedom to the workers, he
denied intellectuals the right to feel free of the demands of class
politics, which for a Marxist are a matter of historical necessity. . . .
The working class will be freed by intellectuals who recognize the
yoke of necessity and act in ways predetermined by history. (151)[9]

The irony Diggins identifies helps to explain why the organic intellectual
has not emerged to any thoroughgoing extent and why this ideal cannot be
sustained on Animal Farm. Chantal Mouffe acknowledges this weakness in
Gramsci's theory in a more hopeful tone, "This new development of marxism carried out by the collective intellectual has, so far, not taken place.
Gramsci's project remains a project" (162). His project stands as an ideal
based on the ability of intellectuals to see themselves and their concerns in
relation to those of others within the group instead of separating themselves
as a distinct class. This modest requirement is all Gramsci's theory asks of
the intellectual. *Animal Farm* dramatizes the myriad reasons why such a
seemingly simple requirement has eluded realization.

Dante Germino's words, meant to defend Gramsci against his critics,
may also be used to defend the importance of decency to Orwell:

Realists and pragmatists will discuss Gramsci as an idealist.
'Pessimism of the intellect and optimism of the will' was his motto,
however, and his understanding of politics as the theory and
practice of overcoming emargination—and re-emargination—is
more complete, more subtle, and more just than are most other
images of politics current today. (265)

Germino's mentioning of a more just image of politics resonates clearly in
the context of Orwell's vision of the pigs' betrayal of decency in favor of
self-interest.

Patrick Reilly describes Orwell using the same formulation Germino
uses to describe Gramsci. Reilly's complete statement on the Gramsci connection usefully qualifies what many have seen as a pessimism in Orwell's
writing: "Orwell himself never ceased to dream, however guardedly and with
prophylactic self-derision, of the just society which he had seen flower briefly
in Barcelona; like Gramsci, he combined pessimism of the intelligence with
optimism of the will. Because things are not as we wish doesn't entail capitu-
lation to them as they are: if we cannot get what we like, must we like what
we get? If freedom is a dream, must we love the jailer?" (*Age's Adversary* 246).
Germino and Reilly make clear the underlying benefit of a focus on decency,

even within the world Orwell creates in *Animal Farm*: just because we face certain, possibly even vicious opposition, we need not give up hope that things might always improve.

* * *

Gramsci's theory of the organic intellectual is very important as it relates to the behavior of the pigs, since one of their first actions after Jones is over-thrown, even before the harvest is taken in, is to keep for themselves "five buckets of frothing creamy milk at which many of the animals looked with considerable interest" (16). After this first selfish decision is taken by the pigs, they need to rely upon their superior rhetorical skills in order to divert the others' attention away from the promise of fresh milk:

> 'What is going to happen to all that milk?' said someone.
> 'Jones used sometimes to mix some of it in our mash,' said one of the hens.
> 'Never mind the milk, comrades!' cried Napoleon, placing himself in front of the buckets. 'That will be attended to. The harvest is more important. Comrade Snowball will lead the way. I shall follow in a few minutes. Forward, comrades! The hay is waiting.'
> So the animals trooped down to the hayfield to begin the harvest, and when they came back in the evening it was noticed that the milk had disappeared. (16)

Napoleon efficiently invokes the larger goals of the farm—to harvest the hay—to distract the animals from the short-term treat of milk. The "direc-tive" function of the intellectuals works in this scene to the direct detriment of the emergence of decency on the farm overall. That the milk "will be attended to" provides the sort of strategic passive construction of reassurance that is actually intended to keep the listener from listening too closely, just enough diversion to secure the moment necessary for the pigs to collect the milk for themselves, away from the eyes of the busy animals.

The pigs are to function as the farm's intellectuals and leaders after the rebellion, and Squealer produces a tendentious explanation to this effect, pur-porting to explain the pigs' need for the milk by connecting their satisfaction to the overall security of the farm:

> You do not imagine, I hope, that we pigs are doing this in a spirit of selfishness and privilege? Many of us actually dislike milk and

apples. I dislike them myself. Our sole object in taking these things is to preserve our health. Milk and apples (this has been proved by Science, comrades) contain substances absolutely necessary to the well-being of a pig. We pigs are brainworkers. The whole management and organization of this farm depend on us. Day and night we are watching over your welfare. It is for your sake that we drink that milk and eat those apples. Do you know what would happen if we pigs failed in our duty? Jones would come back! Yes, Jones would come back! (23)

Squealer's speech is very clever in its immediate refutation of the counterargument ("selfishness and privilege") followed by ostensible proof of the pigs' selflessness, since he claims that many of them actually dislike milk and apples, as he himself does. Next, he draws the other animals' attention to the pigs' superior intellect with an appeal to science, and also calls his cohort "brainworkers," hence, more important than the other animals and therefore possessed of special dietary requirements that the others could not possibly comprehend. His description of the pigs as managers and organizers even sounds like Gramsci's description of organic intellectuals as constructors, organizers, and persuaders, participating actively in the operation of the farm. The peroration of this short speech appeals again to the pigs' selflessness; the repetition of "your" ("your welfare," "your sake") stresses the pigs' concern for others, not themselves. The speech ends with another repetition, the threat of the worst possible outcome, which might come about if these brainworkers cannot eat the apples and drink the milk—Jones will return. Squealer's speech is a masterwork of duplicity, as he claims to hold only the interests of the other animals at heart and is able to dissimulate in order to consolidate the pigs' self-interest. The pigs' decision to start hording first milk and then apples, as explained by Squealer in a way that makes the pigs sound like the best organic intellectuals, marks the beginning of their betrayal of Gramsci's ideals as well as the rebellion.

The order that goes out in the first days after the rebellion—that all the windfall apples are "to be collected and brought to the harness-room for the use of the pigs" (22)—marks one of the very few times that Snowball and Napoleon agree. Despite the pigs' collective betrayal of the ideals set out by Major, though, Snowball is noticeable in his willingness to lead in the organic way that Gramsci theorized. Snowball organizes the other animals into "Animal Committees" (20); he also explains to the "stupider animals" who have difficulty learning to read that the seven commandments of Animalism can be reduced to the single maxim, "Four legs good, two legs bad" (21). These actions suggest a belief in inclusion rather than elitism on Snowball's part. He attempts overall to *function* as an intellectual within and for the animals and attempts to treat the others decently.

In addition to his theoretical work, though, when Jones gathers a few men to attack the farm, Snowball is prominent and active in organizing the animals so they can protect their newly won territory. This is the active participation in practical life Gramsci sees as the proper role of the intellectual. Snowball "had studied an old book of Julius Caesar's campaigns which he had found in the farmhouse" (26), and so organizes the farm's defensive strategies. He also leads the second wave of the animals' counteroffensive—the first wave being the flock of thirty-five pigeons that "mutes" on the men's heads from the sky and the gaggle of geese that peck at the men's legs. The second wave sees Snowball leading Muriel the goat, Benjamin the donkey, and all the sheep in a charge against the men. During this phase of the counteroffensive, Snowball is wounded by pellets fired from Jones's shotgun. After the "Battle of the Cowshed"—as the confrontation is later named—is won, Snowball makes a speech commemorating the animals' dead and is awarded, along with Boxer, the brand-new military decoration "Animal Hero, First Class." In terms of leadership, organization, and active participation, then, Snowball embodies the spirit of the organic intellectual; and his willingness to think in terms of others' concerns suggests he has a capacity for decency, which stands in sharp contrast to the indecency of Napoleon.

It is finally Snowball's idea that the animals should build a windmill that forces the cold war between himself and Napoleon out into the open. As his introductory description says, Napoleon is a pig of very few words. So, when Snowball introduces the windmill idea at one of the farm's weekly meetings, Napoleon says nothing. He does, however, make his feelings about the windmill abundantly clear: "He walked heavily round the shed, looked closely at every detail of the plans and snuffed at them once or twice, then stood for a little while contemplating them out of the corner of his eye; then suddenly he lifted his leg, urinated over the plans and walked out without uttering a word" (33). Napoleon's gesture—apart from reminding us that these are animals, after all—conveys with unmistakable clarity his disdain for any idea not his own. His narrowness cannot coexist peacefully with Snowball's doubleness.

Consolidating Power and Enforcing the Rules of Indecency

Napoleon's wordless but emphatic registration of his disapproval of Snowball's windmill plan is actually part of Napoleon's larger strategy to establish a cult of personality around himself. Such a cult is definitive of the narrowness that discourages the organic leadership Snowball attempts to implement in the days immediately following Jones's ouster. Whereas Snowball concentrates on reform for the farm as a whole, with each of the animals

contributing "according to his capacity" (18), Napoleon schemes to consolidate power solely for himself. He secretly trains the sheep to break into
choruses of "'Four legs good, two legs bad' at crucial moments in Snowball's
speeches" (32), for instance, recognizing the importance of the slogan as
political instrument.

More important, especially early in his seizing of power, is his foresight
in secreting nine puppies born to Jessie and Bluebell. Here we see again the
duplicity we encountered in Flory, but Napoleon demonstrates as well the
difference in magnitude between the individual failings of a man without
influence and the greater potential for disaster when what is essentially the
same bent for duplicity is seated in someone who can determine the fate of an
entire society. In Flory's case, his progressive-sounding but empty pronouncements regarding the Burmese have the mundane ulterior motives of trying
to impress Elizabeth so that he can gain a wife and of holding himself above
the common run of Englishmen in Kyauktada. Napoleon's duplicity appears
when he first trumpets the value of education, but then cultivates a secret
police force out of Jessie's and Bluebell's puppies. He claims "the education
of the young was more important than anything that could be done for those
who were already grown up" (22). He then takes the puppies from Jessie and
Bluebell as soon as they are weaned, saying he will "make himself responsible
for their education" (22). The puppies disappear just as the milk did earlier.
Napoleon keeps them in such seclusion, in fact, that "the rest of the farm soon
forgot their existence" (22). As it turns out, his apparent altruism in taking on
the puppies' education reveals its true purpose after he urinates on Snowball's
windmill drawings. The sequestering of the puppies, instead of serving the
pigs—the new ruling class—as a whole, as did the milk and then the apples,
serves just one pig, the new dictator.

When Napoleon finally makes his grab for power, the farm is changed
irrevocably. As Snowball sketches out his plan for the windmill, which he now
expansively envisions producing enough electricity to operate "threshing-
machines, ploughs, harrows, rollers and reapers and binders, besides supplying
every stall with its own electric light, hot and cold water and an electric heater"
(35)—demonstrating one last time the breadth of his willingness to take others' concerns into account—Napoleon stands up and utters "a high-pitched
whimper of a kind no one had ever heard him utter before" (35). From a place
where decency still exists as a possible basis for leadership, the farm turns, in an
instant, into a place where decency is outlawed forever by force:

> At this there was a terrible baying sound outside, and nine
> enormous dogs wearing brass-studded collars came bounding into
> the barn. They dashed straight for Snowball, who only sprang from

his place just in time to escape their snapping jaws. In a moment he was out of the door and they were after him. . . . Suddenly he slipped and it seemed certain that they had him. Then he was up again, running faster than ever, then the dogs were gaining on him again. One of them all but closed his jaws on Snowball's tail, but Snowball whisked it free just in time. Then he put on an extra spurt and, with a few inches to spare, slipped through a hole in the hedge and was seen no more. (35–36)

As the animals watch in horror, the dogs return to Napoleon's side, and "they wagged their tails to him in the same way as the other dogs had been used to do to Mr. Jones" (36). The direct association of Napoleon with Jones, the animals' deposed enemy, announces the shift in the farm's political future. And just as Jones did not care about the interests of the animals, it becomes clear very quickly that Napoleon shares this same self-centered blindness. Moreover, the farm is worse off than before the rebellion, since now the enemy who rules the farm is one of them. Further still, at least the prospect of decency as a guiding principle existed in the idealized future Major described when Jones still ran things. Once Napoleon takes over, it becomes clear that decency as a determining principle no longer exists as part of the animals' future.

One of the most obvious changes to power relations on the farm is that instead of working in the interest of the pigs as a class, as he did when he first explained why the pigs had to keep the apples and the milk to themselves, Squealer now works exclusively in the service of Napoleon. After Snowball is exiled from the farm, Squealer must explain that Napoleon has made a great personal sacrifice in taking on the extra burden of leadership by himself: "Do not imagine, comrades, that leadership is a pleasure! On the contrary, it is a deep and heavy responsibility" (37). The consolidation of Napoleon's power requires more than an explanation for his leadership; it requires that Snowball's memory be sullied by Squealer in favor of Napoleon:

> 'No one believes more firmly than Comrade Napoleon that all animals are equal. He would be only too happy to let you make your own decisions for yourselves. But sometimes you might make the wrong decisions, comrades, and then where should we be? Suppose you had decided to follow Snowball, with his moonshine of windmills—Snowball, who, as we now know, was no better than a criminal?' (37)

And so, Napoleon's revisionist story begins, with the help of the skilled propagandist Squealer, who makes sure that the animals understand the correct history, the only acceptable version of history. From here, Squealer can 'explain' that Snowball was in fact a coward who had hidden in the background while *Napoleon* charged bravely forward during the Battle of the Cowshed, yelling "Death to Humanity!" (54), no less, another mental image the animals cannot seem to retrieve from their own memories until Squealer 'reminds' them. The animals are also reminded that the windmill was in fact Napoleon's idea all along and that it may now be completed since the traitor Snowball has been banished. Snowball, the potential organic intellectual who carried within his ideas for the farm many possible benefits to the other animals, becomes, in stark contrast to what might have been, nothing more than a ready-made scapegoat, whose putative treachery can be used to explain away any ill fortune that befalls the farm, such as the first collapse of the windmill as a result of a severe storm.

The well-known revisions of the seven commandments of Animalism also represent how decency is outlawed incrementally under Napoleon's regime. The principle underlying Animalism is summarized in the seventh commandment—"All animals are equal." But the other six commandments also inscribe for the farm a rule of decency in the animals' treatment of one another, which includes but is not limited to equality. The commandments are also intended, as Major said, to point up humanity's vices and remind the animals what activities specifically are to be avoided. As the story progresses, though, anytime Napoleon treads upon the tenets of decency comprised in the seven commandments—whether by living inside the once-forbidden farmhouse, sleeping in a bed, drinking alcohol, or engaging in trade, in short, all of the prohibitions Major mentioned in the days before the rebellion[10]—the rules are retroactively brought into line with the only acceptable way of seeing the world, that of Napoleon. The final bastardization of Animalism: "ALL ANIMALS ARE EQUAL, BUT SOME ANIMALS ARE MORE EQUAL, THAN OTHERS" (90),[11] sums up the roles of duplicity and propaganda, as well as the character of the indecency perpetrated by the pigs on the other animals. The vestige of the original commandment ("all animals are equal") that remains in the revised version of Animalism mocks the non-pigs on the farm as it does the progenitor of Animalism, Old Major. The revised version of Animalism has effectively outlawed decency and now works entirely in the interest of Napoleon and those pigs who serve him.

Boxer and Decency's Final Demise

If history teaches us nothing else, it teaches that force must occasionally support propaganda in order to maintain an unjust regime. It is always possible that simply insisting upon the singular will of the ruler may not be enough to keep everyone from stumbling upon a point of view that might arrive at better solutions or at least pose awkward questions which the ruler cannot answer. Therefore, when the effectiveness of indoctrination falters, as it occasionally will, coercion always remains a convenient alternative. The purges Napoleon conducts after he hears of Boxer's resistance to his revisions of Snowball's contribution to the Battle of the Cowshed are crucial to the movement from the optimism and exhilaration that follow the rebellion to the dawning despair of Napoleon's dictatorship.

Napoleon has numerous animals, including four pigs, torn apart by his attack dogs, "until there was a pile of corpses lying before Napoleon's feet and the air was heavy with the smell of blood, which had been unknown there since the expulsion of Jones" (57). The executions leave the other animals "shaken and miserable" (57). They cannot decide which is more shocking, "the treachery of the animals who had leagued themselves with Snowball" (57)—the stated reason for the purges—"or the cruel retribution they had just witnessed" (57). For the purposes of Napoleon's regime, it is crucial that all the animals witness the slaughter. The show-trial nature of these executions ensures Napoleon that the other animals see the potentially dire consequences of his power and understand that even if they hold alternate views of the world in which they live, they should not, under any circumstances, give voice to them. Furthermore, the fact that four pigs are slaughtered shows the animals that no one—not even members of the preferred class—is immune to swift and severe punishment. This aspect of the purge also makes clear that power is less and less about the pigs as a class and more about Napoleon as a singular tyrant.

* * *

The inverse relationship between monomania and decency as well as the importance of force in supporting a narrow and self-serving version of history find their clearest expressions in the novella in Boxer's death. Interestingly, the pigs' use of force in getting rid of the increasingly problematic carthorse also portends the eventual demise of Napoleon's regime.

Boxer is the most decent character in the story, a fact indicated repeatedly in the narrative. His first appearance is marked by how he (along with Clover, the other horse) puts down his vast hooves "with great care lest there should be some small animal concealed in the straw" (2), as the animals assemble to hear Major's speech. Boxer's defining trait from the beginning of the story is his selfless care for others. In fact, he is devastated when, during the Battle of the Cowshed, he thinks he has killed one of the men who attack the farm: "'I have no wish to take life, not even human life,' repeated Boxer, and his eyes were full of tears" (28). As it turns out, the man is only stunned by Boxer's hoof and escapes the farm as soon as he regains consciousness, but Boxer's reaction to the thought that his strength might have cost someone else—even a human being—his life is almost more than his sense of decency can bear.

On the farm, Boxer's selflessness is most obvious through his capacity for hard work. As a result of his physical strength but also his seemingly limitless capacity for work, he is the object of admiration of the other animals, particularly in the first days after the rebellion:

> He had been a hard worker even in Jones's time, but now he seemed more like three horses than one; there were days when the entire work of the farm seemed to rest upon his mighty shoulders. From morning to night he was pushing and pulling, always at the spot where the work was hardest. He had made an arrangement with one of the cockerels to call him in the mornings half an hour earlier than anyone else, and would put in some volunteer labour at whatever seemed to be most needed, before the regular day's work began. His answer to every problem, every setback, was 'I will work harder!'—which he had adopted as his personal motto. (18)

Boxer's temperament as a selfless and tireless worker for the cause makes him the embodiment of the best of Major's revolutionary vision.

But as the physical representation of the good that Major envisioned for the animals after the overthrow of humanity, Boxer cannot be allowed to stay on the farm. His admirable presence is too much a potential contradiction to the singular, self-absorbed vision of Napoleon. More importantly, though, his propensity for remembering what has already been said becomes an irritant to the pigs. When Squealer asserts that Snowball was "in league with Jones from the very start" (53) and was actually Jones's secret agent, this is too much for Boxer—"who seldom asked questions" (54) to this point in the story—to bear: "'I do not believe that,' he said. 'Snowball fought bravely at the Battle of the Cowshed. I saw him myself. Did we not give him 'Animal Hero, First Class' immediately afterwards?'" (54). Boxer is motivated by a desire to respect Snowball's memory even though he is no longer on the farm. The carthorse appeals to his own recollections, to what he saw for himself, in defending the departed Snowball. The awarding of the medal is particularly easy for Boxer to remember since he too was awarded the then-newly invented medal along with Snowball.

This disagreement between Squealer and Boxer on the correct version of the animals' ever-changing history finally forces the two worldviews—the singular and the doubled—into direct conflict in front of the other animals. Squealer's revised account of the Battle of the Cowshed leaves Boxer feeling "a little uneasy" (55) as the discussion continues, and Squealer finally puts Boxer's arguments to rest by appealing to the horse's obedient, selfless nature:

> 'Our Leader, Comrade Napoleon,' announced Squealer, speaking very slowly and firmly, 'has stated categorically—categorically, comrade—that Snowball was Jones's agent from the very beginning—yes, and from long before the Rebellion was ever thought of.' (55)

This is Squealer's rhetorical *coup de grâce*, since he knows Boxer will always accede to the wishes of Napoleon, "'Ah, that is different!' said Boxer. 'If Comrade Napoleon says it, it must be right'" (55). While this ends the argument for the moment, it is noticed[12] that Squealer "cast a very ugly look at Boxer with his little twinkling eyes" (55). The disagreement between Squealer and the usually obedient Boxer signals to Squealer, and then to Napoleon, that Boxer's ability to remember and articulate a version of events that is different from the version endorsed (and enforced) by Napoleon is not commensurable with the narrow interests of the dictatorship.

Not surprisingly, then, little time passes between this scene and the pigs' first attempt to set things right by force. Only four days after the disagreement between Boxer and Squealer on Snowball's role in the Battle of the Cowshed, the purges take place. To everyone's amazement three of Napoleon's dogs descend upon Boxer. But in attacking Boxer, Napoleon's force meets with an even more imposing resistance:

> Boxer saw them coming and put out his great hoof, caught a dog in midair, and pinned him to the ground. The dog shrieked for mercy and the other two fled with their tails between their legs. Boxer looked at Napoleon to know whether he should crush the dog to death or let it go. Napoleon appeared to change countenance, and sharply ordered Boxer to let the dog go, whereat Boxer lifted his hoof, and the dog slunk away, bruised and howling. (56)

Even in this moment, when Boxer is attacked by Napoleon's dogs, he looks to Napoleon for guidance. As with the man whom he injures in the Battle of the Cowshed, he cannot bring himself—of his own volition—to cause harm to another. But in effortlessly subduing the dogs, he also identifies himself as not easily controlled by Napoleon's singular will. To be rid of Boxer, then, Napoleon will need outside help.

The significance of Squealer's "ugly look" at Boxer after their argument over Snowball's role in the rebellion finally manifests itself in Boxer's destruction after he collapses under the combined burdens of his workload and his advancing years. As his twelfth birthday approaches and with a windmill to rebuild after the second attack on the farm by Frederick (one of the neighboring farmers) and his men, Boxer finally cannot go on, and it is only here that his thoughts—for the first and only time in the novella—turn to himself. As Boxer lies on his side, unable to raise his head, Clover asks him what is wrong,

> 'It is my lung,' said Boxer in a weak voice. 'It does not matter. I think you will be able to finish the windmill without me. There is a pretty good store of stone accumulated. I had only another month to go in any case. To tell you the truth, I had been looking forward to my retirement. And perhaps, as Benjamin is growing old too, they will let him retire at the same time and be a companion to me.' (80)

Boxer still believes that the pigs will hold to the policy they announced earlier that there would be a part of the pasture set aside for animals too old to work. But, of course, we are past the point when such decent treatment for the aged is to be expected. His weakened state is an opportunity the pigs cannot let slip by.

When it is announced that Boxer is to be sent to a hospital off the farm the animals find this news disquieting. The pigs contrive to have the horse taken away while the other animals are in the field working and when they discover he is leaving it is too late to do anything but shout goodbye to him from a distance. This is the moment when Benjamin, who has known how to read since the animals were first taught but has steadfastly refused to do so, speaks up and reads the words on the side of the "ambulance" to the others: "'Alfred Simmonds, Horse Slaughterer and Glue Boiler, Willingdon. Dealer in Hides and Bone-Meal. Kennels Supplied.' Do you not understand what that means? They are taking Boxer to the knacker's!" (82). The pigs have finally found their opportunity to rid themselves of the main source of competition to their version of reality. Boxer's dismissal, with the explanation that he will receive better treatment at the hospital in Willingdon, enables the pigs to reinscribe their singular perspective on the farm once and for all.

Once the carthorse is taken away, the wheels of propaganda can begin to turn again, as force from the outside (in the form of the knacker's wagon) assists the ongoing imposition of Napoleon's will. First, Squealer announces to the other animals that Boxer is dead, providing an account of Boxer's last days that is equal parts melodrama and ideological correctness:

> 'It was the most affecting sight I have ever seen!' said Squealer, lifting his trotter and wiping away a tear. 'I was at his bedside at the

very last. And at the end, almost too weak to speak, he whispered in my ear that his sole sorrow was to have passed on before the windmill was finished. "Forward comrades!" he whispered. "Forward in the name of the Rebellion. Long live Animal Farm! Long live Comrade Napoleon! Napoleon is always right." Those were his very last words, comrades.' (83)

Boxer's well-known selflessness is available to help the pigs' own selfish cause, as his motto "Napoleon is always right" can be used in the service of indecency. The slaughtering of the most admirable comrade of the group is transformed into a duplicitous example of Napoleon's benevolent leadership.

But the pigs' version of history must also address the matter of the words written on the side of the wagon that took Boxer away, words made all the more memorable to the animals for having been read aloud to them by the always intransigent—and largely silent—Benjamin. In addressing this question, Squealer's "demeanour suddenly changed. He fell silent for a moment, and his little eyes darted suspicious glances from side to side before he proceeded" (83). These side-to-side glances are reminiscent of the "ugly look" Squealer casts upon Boxer when he dares to ask too many questions about the official version of events. Squealer tells the gathered animals that there is a "very simple" explanation why Benjamin saw the words "horse slaughterer" on the side of the van: "The van had previously been the property of the knacker, and had been bought by the veterinary surgeon, who had not yet painted the old name out. That was how the mistake had arisen" (83). This convenient explanation leaves the animals "enormously relieved" (83) and assuages the lingering suspicions about Napoleon's motivations. One of the effects of power is that the might attached to one's perceived status lends added authority even to the most implausible pronouncements. After all, to question Napoleon, as the animals know, is to put oneself at risk. This is the privilege Squealer is able to rely upon and exercise on Napoleon's behalf.

Boxer's elimination and the recuperation of his story in the interest of the dictator provide a neat example of how the repressive state apparatus, as described by Louis Althusser, works.

Remember that in Marxist theory, the State Apparatus (SA) contains: the Government, the Administration, the Army, the Police, the Courts, the Prisons, etc., which constitute what I shall in future call the Repressive State Apparatus. Repressive suggests that the State Apparatus in question 'functions by violence'—at least ultimately (since repression, e.g. administrative repression, may take non-physical forms). (142–43)[13]

In the microcosm Orwell creates on Manor Farm, the repressive state apparatus is concentrated in essentially three forms: the government (Napoleon), the administration (Squealer), and the police (the dogs). We might also include the courts in the form of the show trials and purges, but that is essentially another manifestation of Napoleon as government. All of the power of the new state is brought to bear in order to be rid of Boxer. As the repressive state apparatus works here in the interest of Napoleon's official version of history, the farm now exists solely under the influence of one account of events, sanctioned and enforced by its dictator.

Decency and Justice—Is Behaving Decently a Mark of Weakness?

Three additional important points emerge from Boxer's death. The first has to do with the significance of the pigs resorting to an outside agency in order to rid themselves of his persistent, and, for the pigs, inconveniently doubled point of view. The second is concerned with the nature of his decency that emerges from the story. Lastly, the question remains: what does Orwell's depiction of the fate of decency in *Animal Farm* say about the viability of this value in general?

On the first point: it is tempting to see Napoleon's power on the farm as absolute by the end of the novella. Napoleon desires that Animal Farm "live at peace and in normal business relations" (93) with its neighbors, as he tells the gathering of men and pigs at the conclusion of the story. For this reason he changes the farm's name back to "Manor Farm," outlaws animals calling one another "comrade," and changes the flag from the hoof and horn—symbolic of the animals' rebellion—to a politically neutral plain green field. Obviously, "normal business relations" are meant to benefit the pigs and their canine enforcers, and no other animals. The pigs envisage themselves on an equal footing with the humans, as they attempt to prove by teaching themselves to walk upright. They are heralded and promoted above the level of the other animals and, with tentative unsure steps, to the level of humans by the new slogan, "Four legs good, two legs *better*!" (89). This scene is reminiscent of the joyous days immediately after the rebellion, when the pigs are made the butt of an innocent and charming joke as they paint the seven commandments of Animalism on a barn wall: "With some difficulty (for it is not easy for a pig to balance himself on a ladder) Snowball climbed up and set to work, with Squealer a few rungs below him holding the paint-pot" (15). This early light-hearted image of two pigs balancing precariously on a ladder provides some perspective on just how low the lofty hopes for the rebellion have sunk by the end of the fable. A comic image of animals awkwardly overcoming their physical limitations in the interest of the common good becomes the mark of the pigs' final indecency at the expense of the other animals, and of the pigs' desire to be just like the species they originally overthrew because of its indecency towards them. The final dispute at the card game shows a balance as shaky as a pig standing on its hind legs and hints at future trouble for the long-term health of the animals' rebellion.

The pigs' attempt to mimic the human ability to walk upright hints at their greater vulnerability and the irony that works against their interest as the story ends. One is always in a position of disadvantage when trying to imitate the original. When the pigs attempt to approximate the upright orientation of the human being, they betray their own future weakness, a weakness expressed literally in the instability of their first steps. But more than this, even if they improve their facility for moving around on two legs instead of four, they will always be little more than an awkward imitation of the real thing, instead of becoming something wholly new and quite possibly better, in the manner described by Major and envisioned by Snowball.

The eventual defeat of Napoleon is also implied by the increasing severity of the attacks the farm endures. The first time the farm is attacked, Jones brings his four men along with "half a dozen others from Foxwood and Pinchfield" (26), the two neighboring farms. The men carry sticks, all except Jones "who was marching ahead with a gun in his hands" (26). The men, understandably, expect to be able to take back the farm by the sheer force of being human. They do not expect the level of organization and tactics the animals exhibit under Snowball's tutelage, and underestimate the animals' ability to protect their property. As a result, the men lose this first clash.

When they attack the second time, however, the men are fifteen strong, "with half a dozen guns between them, and they opened fire as soon as they got within fifty yards" (68). They also bring with them enough dynamite to destroy the windmill, the walls of which are three feet thick and made of stone. While Squealer insists on a celebration of their victory after the men leave the farm the second time—a claim that leads to another argument with Boxer[14]—it is clear that the men can keep bringing more and more force to bear on the farm as is needed. The animals will have no adequate reply in the face of this increased force. As the story ends, then, and the pigs and men drink toasts to the newly renamed "Manor Farm" and sit down to a game of cards, the joke is on Napoleon and the other pigs, since it is just a matter of time before the farm is defeated irrevocably by the humans.

There can be no real trust between the new business partners, irrespective of Napoleon's pronouncements. As both Napoleon and Pilkington each play an ace of spades simultaneously at the card game and a violent quarrel ensues, the new alliance's days are already numbered. Orwell's explanation of the allegory of the Russian Revolution helps explain further the significance of the pigs' future defeat:

> A number of readers may finish the book with the impression that
> it ends in the complete reconciliation of the pigs and the humans.
> That was not my intention; on the contrary I meant it to end on a
> loud note of discord, for I wrote it immediately after the Teheran
> Conference which everybody thought had established the best
> possible relations between the USSR and the West. I personally did
> not believe that such good relations would last long; and, as events
> have shown, I wasn't far wrong. (19.89)

The loud note of discord, though, also sounds the beginning of the end
of Napoleon's reign on the farm. When we remember that the human
beings can always amass sufficient force to overpower the animals at any
time—they can also cheat them, as shown when Mr. Whymper gives the
pigs counterfeit money in exchange for very real timber from the farm—it
must be said that the pigs' hold on power is tenuous at best in relation to the
world outside the farm.

A sense of escalation is also evident in the manner in which the pigs
exile first Snowball and then Boxer from the farm. Like the implied threat
of increasing armaments that can be rallied against the farm by the human
farmers in the area, this second image of escalation also weighs against Napoleon's ability to maintain his dictatorship. When Napoleon finally makes his
grab for power early in the story, he can simply call out his attack dogs and
rely upon the element of surprise in getting rid of Snowball. When he wants
to rid himself of Boxer, though, he must make more than one attempt, since
the carthorse is more difficult to overpower than his rival among the pigs
was. The suggestion in this bit of escalation is that the effort it takes to get rid
of dissenting animals may also continue to increase and that dissenters will
always emerge even from within an oppressed population. Perhaps at some
point, the dictator will no longer be able to simply overpower dissenters and
the prospect for decency may return. Orwell's insertion of a "loud note of
discord" extends beyond the bounds of the original allegory to an application
more topical to the early twenty-first century. The hopeful message of the
end of *Animal Farm* according to the criteria of doubleness and decency is
that the oppression of a subject people cannot last forever and will always be
resisted by the force of decency.

These two examples of escalation imply that a mitigated optimism
emerges from the outcome of the story. While it is true that Napoleon, with
the help of the other pigs, rules the farm as the novella ends, hope resides in
the fact that their indecency will inevitably be overcome. They will eventually get their comeuppance. If not the socialist utopia foretold by Major, and
if not the common decency that underlies Orwell's brand of socialism, this,

at least, is a promise of justice, or at least revenge against the indecent, who will not prevail. The human force that threatens to overthrow the pigs would, of course, return all the animals to the level of servitude they endured under Jones, possibly worse, since an added vigilance would be the order of the day when human beings retook the farm, in order to make sure that there were no more insurrections. As a new oppression by humans will eventually supplant oppression by the pigs, one force of indecency appears to replace another. The pigs will be beaten at their own game—another lesson in the risks inherent in imitation, which Major warned against from the beginning. So, while the pigs get their just deserts, this projected outcome would leave the rest of the animals no better off than before the rebellion. This is hardly surprising since subject groups often pay for the mistakes of the privileged. But this projected conclusion to Napoleon's dictatorship also serves as a warning to future revolutionaries to remain faithful to the precepts of their cause and be wary of possible indecencies.

The second point that emerges from Boxer's death has to do with the nature of his decency. Boxer has difficulty in thinking things out for himself. Once he accepts the pigs as his teachers, consonant with their positioning as the intellectuals and leaders of the farm, he absorbs everything he is told and "passe[s] it on to the other animals by simple arguments" (11). The decency that manifests itself in Boxer's concern for others does not equip him to look critically at the potential effects of the pigs' actions on his own best interests.[15] What makes Boxer so admirable, then, also makes him most vulnerable to the unscrupulous pigs. He devotes himself unwittingly to their exclusive interests and his own destruction while intending to work for the farm as a whole. He is incapable of discerning this opposition of interests in part because he is repeatedly told that what is good for Napoleon is good for the farm. His personal mottos, "I will work harder" and "Napoleon is always right," are vows of loyalty, of course, but they also mark his weakest point. Whereas his decency is admired and appreciated by the other animals, it is recognized and seized upon by the pigs.

A similar susceptibility to exploitation may be seen in Veraswami and Rosemary. In *Burmese Days*, Veraswami can be humiliated by Flory, who signs the petition calling the doctor and the other Burmese "niggers," because Veraswami is too much of a dedicated friend to put Flory in the awkward position that would arise if Veraswami were to insist upon the apology to which as a human being he is clearly entitled, even if the rules of colonialism say otherwise. Veraswami's concessions to Flory are of a different character than Ravelston's with respect to Gordon in *Aspidistra* inasmuch as Ravelston knows that Gordon's anti-money position is fallacious and says nothing. Veraswami, by contrast, believes in Flory's goodness as a human being, so he is acting in keeping with his beliefs when he refuses to ask anything more of Flory than he knows Flory can do when it comes to matters regarding membership in the Club. Rosemary tolerates Gordon's boorish behavior and inflexible views on gender because she is devoted to him and, like Julia, Gordon's sister, has had inculcated into her the rules of her time that state a woman must concede her interests to a man's. It is the existence of this social convention, and her consciousness of this convention, that makes her contradictions of Ravelston and Gordon all the more remarkable and admirable.

In both cases, then, the decent characters' tolerance is predicated on their willingness to put the principal characters' needs ahead of their own. But this can be done in *Burmese Days* and *Keep the Aspidistra Flying* because, while Veraswami and Rosemary may be seen as exploited or even abused by Flory and Gordon, respectively, they do not live in a world in which such treatment puts them in any real danger. Veraswami is demoted and trans-ferred, it is true, and Rosemary is insulted and subjected on more than one occasion to Gordon's childish obstinacy, but neither is sent to the knacker's or, as is the case with the decent character in Orwell's final novel, to Room 101, to be "cured," to use O'Brien's euphemism for Winston Smith's torture and brainwashing. Rosemary marries Gordon and is expecting a child as that novel ends. She also now has the promise that her new husband will begin to behave more like an adult. Decency means vulnerability on the individual level of personal inconvenience or disappointment in the first two novels, whereas it means a life-or-death risk when faced with a totalitarian power structure whose ambitions run directly counter to the concerns, ideas, or well being of others, as in the last two novels. Those who do not comply with the demands of the overarching structure will be eliminated or "cured."

In addition to his incapacity to act selfishly at all, Boxer's decency ren-ders him vulnerable in another way as well. He is instrumental in Napoleon's quest to secure his power on the farm by making the construction of the windmill possible. It is difficult to imagine the windmill being completed "to the very day" (66) Napoleon set as a target without Boxer's vast and selfless contributions. The significance of the windmill to Napoleon is made explicit when, upon its completion, he names it after himself. Napoleon overworks Boxer for his own selfish purposes and then cruelly discards him.

The significance to the pigs of Boxer's doubled perspective is also indicated in the novella's structure, in the nature of the horses who replace him. Once Boxer is sent away, the story shifts to years later, and a farm on which "there was no one who remembered the old days before the Rebel-lion, except Clover, Benjamin, Moses the raven, and a number of the pigs" (85). By this point, many of the other animals are dead, and Snowball and Boxer have been forgotten. The farm now has three new horses: "They were fine upstanding beasts, willing workers and good comrades, but very stupid. None of them proved able to learn the alphabet beyond the letter B. They accepted everything that they were told about the Rebellion and the principles of Animalism, especially from Clover, for whom they had an almost filial respect; but it was doubtful whether they understood very much of it" (86). This description of the new horses draws to mind the earlier account of Boxer's futile attempts to learn the alphabet, and shows these new horses as much less intelligent even than Boxer was, since they cannot get past the letter B. Boxer

> would trace out A, B, C, D in the dust with his great hoof, and then would stand staring at the letters with his ears back, sometimes shaking his forelock, trying with all his might to remember what came next and never succeeding. On several occasions, indeed, he did learn E, F, G, H, but by the time he knew them it was always discovered that he had forgotten A, B, C and D. Finally he decided to be content with the first four letters, and used to write them out once or twice every day to refresh his memory. (21)

These new horses, then, appear to be less of a threat to the pigs' regime, since they are even less intelligent than the horse the pigs have eliminated. They also understand less of the subtleties of Animalism than did Boxer. The description of the new horses provides a further poignancy as we reflect upon the betrayal of the principles of Animalism, since the description of the horses' struggles with the alphabet brings to mind Boxer's plans for his retirement, his desire to "devote the rest of his life to learning the remaining twenty-two letters of the alphabet" (81). These new horses appear ill equipped to keep in mind anything other than what they are told. As such, they are—from the pigs' point of view—a marked improvement on Boxer since they will not bring any alternative perspective to the farm.

The third and final point that arises from Boxer's death is the question: what does Orwell's choice to depict the fate of the most decent character as he does in *Animal Farm* say about the value in general? His own words help answer the question. An "As I Please" column he wrote in 1946 is one place where Orwell states his simultaneous pessimism of the intellect and optimism of the will:

> When one considers how things have gone since 1930 or thereabouts, it is not easy to believe in the survival of civilisation. I do not argue from this that the only thing to do is to abjure practical politics, or retire to some remote place and concentrate

either on individual salvation or on building up self-supporting communities against the day when the atom bombs have done their work. I think one must continue the political struggle, just as a doctor must try to save the life of a patient who is probably going to die. (18.503)

He uses a very similar construction in his essay "Toward European Unity," published in *Partisan Review* the following year:

A Socialist today is in the position of a doctor treating an all but hopeless case. As a doctor, it is his duty to keep the patient alive, and therefore to assume that the patient has at least a chance of recovery. As a scientist, it is his duty to face the facts, and therefore to admit that the patient will probably die. Our activities as socialists only have meaning if we assume that socialism *can* be established, but if we stop to consider what probably *will* happen, then we must admit, I think, that the chances are against us. (19.163)[16]

Orwell's pessimistic optimism satisfies the criterion for a first-rate intelligence, as F. Scott Fitzgerald sets it out in his 1936 essay, "The Crack-Up": "Before I go on with this short history, let me make a general observation—the test of a first-rate intelligence is the ability to hold two opposed ideas in the mind at the same time, and still retain the ability to function. One should, for example, be able to see that things are hopeless and yet be determined to make them otherwise" (69).[17] More succinctly still, Ellison's narrator in *Invisible Man*, reflecting on the travails that make up his story, concludes that "humanity is won by continuing to play in face of certain defeat" (577). Whether a struggle or a test, then, one can only be truly optimistic, in Orwell's view, if one knows that things can, and in fact, may, turn out badly.

But knowing that events may go against one's wishes is no cause to give up hope. In the simultaneity of knowing both possibilities is the test of the first-rate intelligence, the victory of humanity. In Boxer, Orwell dramatizes this difficult-to-enact ideal. Even though Boxer is defeated by the pigs, he represents what is best in the possibility of decency as an ideal, irrespective of the consequences. Boxer is not diminished in the slightest by the fact that he is sent off the farm to be killed. In fact, if anything, we admire him all the more because of this fact. The extremity of the contrast between the pigs' conduct and that of the carthorse makes crystal clear the preferable course of action, again, irrespective of the consequences. By setting up Boxer against the will of a tyrannical leader, Orwell's story situates the implications and risks inherent in the value of decency in a much broader context than is the case in either of the earlier novels.

* * *

The significance of the decent character and the reasons for this character's actions are both crucial at this point in the trajectory from *Burmese Days* through *Animal Farm*, because once we arrive at *Nineteen Eighty-Four* there is little hope other than that of the emergence of the decent character. Winston Smith is willing to risk everything he has in order to remain "human." The notion of continuing to play in the face of certain defeat encapsulates Winston's relationship with the Inner Party and demonstrates, finally, the value of decency at its most elemental, as an ennobling good in and of itself, irrespective of one's political environment or hopes for victory. It is his capacity for decency, after all, that O'Brien attempts to take from Winston.

Notes

1. Richard Rees tells a story that suggests Orwell did pick up some knowledge of Marxist theory at some point during his life:

> It is true that in the summer of 1936, some months before he went to Spain, he had attended a Summer School organised by *The Adelphi*, where he astonished everybody, including the Marxist theoreticians, by his interventions in the discussions. Without any parade of learning he produced breathtaking Marxist paradoxes and epigrams, in such a way as to make the sacred mysteries seem almost too obvious and simple. At one of the sessions I noticed a leading Marxist eyeing him with a mixture of admiration and uneasiness. (147)

Rees's story might be greatly improved by divulging the identity of the "leading Marxist" whom Orwell so impressed, nor does he explain any further what these "paradoxes and epigrams" consisted of. But the image of Orwell countering theory in the presence of Marxist theoreticians suggests again that his principal interest in socialists was not intellectual conversation as such nor acceptance within a specific group, but the sometimes insurmountable discord between theory and practice. In the end, he was always more interested in practice.

2. Peter Stansky and William Abrahams draw a similar line in the chronology of Orwell's work, although their emphasis is the distinction between the writer's interest first in class and then in human freedom, as opposed to Slater's observation of a transition from concerns about money to concerns about power:

> . . . as a young writer he was fascinated as well as embittered by the class question: it figures obsessively in much of what he wrote before 1936, in the novels, *A Clergyman's Daughter* and *Keep the Aspidistra Flying*, and in the autobiographical portions of *The Road to Wigan*

Pier. It is only in 1937 with *Homage to Catalonia*, his account of his experience in the Spanish Civil War, that he gets beyond it to what would be his principal concern thereafter: human freedom. (4)

3. Jeffrey Meyers provides a thorough account of the allegorical detail at play in the novella:

> Virtually every detail has political significance in this allegory of corruption, betrayal and tyranny in Communist Russia. The human beings are capitalists, the animals are Communists, the wild creatures who could not be tamed are the peasants, the pigs are the Bolsheviks, the Rebellion is the October Revolution, the neighboring farmers are the Western armies who attempted to support the Czarists against the Reds, the waves of rebelliousness that ran through the countryside afterwards are the abortive revolutions in Hungary and Germany in 1919 and 1923, the hoof and horn is the hammer and sickle, the Spontaneous Demonstration is the May Day Celebration, the Order of the Green Banner is the Order of Lenin, the special pigs committee presided over by Napoleon is the Politburo, the revolt of the hens—the first rebellion since the expulsion of Jones (the Czar)—is the sailors' rebellion at Kronstadt naval base in 1921, Napoleon's dealings with Whymper and the Willingdon markets represent the Treaty of Rapallo, signed with Germany in 1922, which ended the capitalists' boycott of Soviet Russia, and the final meeting of the pigs and human beings is the Teheran Conference of 1943. Orwell allegorizes three crucial political events: the disastrous results of Stalin's forced collectivization (1923–33), the Great Purge Trials (1936–38) and the cynical diplomacy with Germany that terminated with Hitler's invasion of Russia in 1941. (249)

4. While it has been pointed out that Old Major's speech is "modelled very much on the concluding section of the Communist Manifesto" (Ingle 76), it should also be said that the possibility of the pigs' emerging as they do in *Animal Farm* is actually presaged by Marx and Engels. The communists are envisioned as

> on the one hand, practically, the most advanced and resolute section of the working-class parties of every country, that section which pushes forward all others; on the other hand, theoretically, they have over the great mass of the proletariat the advantage of clearly understanding the line of march, the conditions, and the ultimate general results of the proletarian movement. (484)

The "on the one hand/on the other hand" construction is an attempt at even-handedness but also conveys the difficult task the manifesto sets for the communists. They should lead without explicitly designating themselves as leaders. Here, obviously, Napoleon parts company with the manifesto's intention, just as he does with Major's, since it is Napoleon's explicit goal to identify the pigs as not only leaders but superior to the other animals and himself as sole leader of all on the farm. The communists are described as part of the working class, but at the same time its "most advanced and resolute section." They are portrayed as *similar* to the rest of the proletariat, but also different in a very fundamental way.

It is clear that the famous manifesto is most often "read for its message," but "the style in which that message is conveyed contributes to the message's effect" (Siegel 222). As important as the intended effect may be the unintended but equally meaningful effect that coexists in the same text. The metaphors that determine the political relationships in the above passage are very telling. The communists are portrayed occupying a position "above" the proletariat. Despite the text's attempts to elide this hierarchical relationship, the image of superiority is left intact. But the text also reconfigures and complicates the conventional horizontal metaphor of leadership. Instead of the communists being *in front* of the proletariat, as the notion of an avant-garde indicates, they are cast in the role of "pushing forward all others." In other words, they are strategically positioned *behind* the proletariat. However, they are still clearly the motivating force, pushing the proletariat forward, providing an impetus for progress that the proletariat, left on its own, would ostensibly lack. The description subtly installs the communists behind the proletariat, but in a way this location merely emphasizes their position of superiority. The communists still have "over" the "great mass" the advantage that they "clearly understand" what the proletariat does not. They are, as Squealer puts it, the "brainworkers." The communists' clear understanding derives from their ability to function as intellectuals in society. The passage perpetuates the two conventional metaphors of leadership, implicitly situating the Communists in front of and above the proletariat.

5. Douglas Kerr emphasizes the importance of the pigs' secrecy as a sign of their superiority over the other animals: "One of the first signs of the ominous kinship between pigs and people is not only the pigs' readiness to interpret and change the world, but also a concomitant ability to keep things to themselves, to nurse a secret mental life of their own, illegible to the entirely outward-oriented and merely bodily horses, sheep and hens" ("Orwell, Animals, and the East" 238). The pigs decide, at this crucial early juncture before the expulsion of Snowball, to oppose selfishly their interests to those of the other animals, explicitly choosing self-interested exclusion over doubleness.

6. Benda defines intellectuals as "all those whose activity essentially is *not* the pursuit of practical aims, all those who seek their joy in the practice of an art or a science or metaphysical speculation, in short in the possession of nonmaterial advantages, and hence in a certain manner say: 'My kingdom is not of this world'" (30).

7. As *The Road to Wigan Pier* rises to its terminal flourish, Orwell mimics *The Communist Manifesto* in order to criticize class-prejudices one last time. He contends that once the members of the proletariat see their common cause with the middle class, "then perhaps this misery of class-prejudice will fade away, and we of the sinking middle class—the private schoolmaster, the half-starved free-lance journalist, the colonel's spinster daughter with £75 a year, the jobless Cambridge graduate, the ship's officer without a ship, the clerks, the civil servants, the commercial travelers and the thrice-bankrupt drapers in the country towns—may sink without further struggles into the working class where we belong, and probably when we get there it will not be so dreadful as we feared, for, after all, we have nothing to lose but our aitches" (215). Orwell's list of déclassé professionals shows a real sensitivity to the disjunction between conventional notions of "class" and function within society. Just as earlier in *Wigan Pier* he describes himself as a member of the bourgeoisie with a working-class income, so here, as he expresses a doubleness of perspective

that enables him to describe how individuals in similarly disjointed positions might better conceive of and contribute to the world around them.

8. In addition to their similar approach to socialism, there are numerous striking biographical coincidences between Orwell and Gramsci. Both were social outcasts (Gramsci was a Sardinian and a hunchback; Orwell as a member of the lower-upper-middle class among the predominantly public-school intelligentsia). Both suffered for most of their lives with tuberculosis (Gramsci was afflicted with Pott's disease, a form of tuberculosis that resulted in his having "two humps, one in front and the other in back, giving him a deformed appearance" [Germino 1]). Both served as journalists, and endured physical hardships in their attempts to develop a new politics. Both were critical of the conventional role of intellectuals and of the specialized language prominent among early twentieth-century socialists. And in perhaps their most striking coincidence, both died at the age of 46. More than anything else, these biographical coincidences are interesting curiosities that no one has noticed before. They are far less important than the similarities in politics evinced by the two men's writings.

9. Writing in *Horizon* (March 1944) specifically in regard to 1930s intellectuals, Arthur Koestler seizes upon a similar irony which he argues determines the function of many intellectuals living under industrialized capitalism: "Their frustrations are repressed, their aspirations are not towards new hierarchies of values, but towards climbing to the top of the existing hierarchy. Thus the intelligentsia, once the vanguard of the ascending bourgeoisie, becomes the Lumpen-Bourgeoisie in the age of its decay" (74). Again, the intellectuals' implication within the structures they attempt to change may actually militate against their effectiveness as agents of change. Koestler reiterates the problematic question of motivation that underlies the doubtfulness of the emergence of an organic intellectual class: "Those who are snugly tucked into the social hierarchy have obviously no strong impulse towards independent thought. Where should it come from? They have no reason to destroy their accepted values nor any desire to build new ones" (73).

10. Regarding the amendments made to each of the tenets of Animalism, Robert Pearce has noticed that "each commandment received a coda, a reservation which effectively reversed its meaning" (66). This reversal explains how the tenets of Animalism can be used by Napoleon against the value of decency. Pearce also notes that the detail of codas suggests no parallel in Russian political history—the conventional referent for Orwell's beast fable—but a parallel in Russian religious history. This suggestion, as part of Pearce's demonstration of what he sees as an influence of Tolstoy upon Orwell, shows that "the provenance of the details of *Animal Farm* is far wider than the painful period of history through which Orwell lived. It is also to contend that Tolstoy was an important influence on Orwell" (67).

11. Anthony Kearney's brief but useful account of this famous expression adds further to our perception of the pigs' betrayal of the sense of decency based on doubleness built into Major's initial vision of life on the farm after the rebellion. Kearney's reading hinges on the fact that if "equal" can mean "something desirable and good, it can also in a primary sense mean no more than 'identical' or 'same'" (238). From here, the less obvious but patently revealing significations of the expression become clear:

> The slogan should read, 'some animals (not the pigs) are more equal (are more the same) than others (the superior pigs).' In this reading

the pigs want less equality, not more; being 'more equal' means that you belong to the common herd, not the elite. In the end this may lead to much the same conclusion as in the popular reading of the slogan—the pigs in both readings are marking themselves off from the other animals—but what is at issue here is the way equality is being defined, by the pigs and of course by Orwell himself. (238)

12. The expression "it was noticed" recurs in the novella. In three early instances "it is noticed" that the milk has disappeared after the animals go to the fields to harvest the first crops after Jones's ouster (16); that Snowball and Napoleon are "never in agreement" (20); and that the sheep "were especially liable to break into 'Four legs good, two legs bad' at crucial moments in Snowball's speeches" (32). The recurrence of this passive construction is as close as the animals can get to the expression of dissenting voices. It becomes increasingly improbable that any animals—but for Boxer—will say anything that does not accord with the pigs' point of view, but the expression "it was noticed" registers that the pigs' transgressions do not entirely escape the other animals.

13. Althusser distinguishes between the repressive state apparatus and the ideological state apparatuses (ISA), in which he includes:

—the religious ISA (the system of the different Churches),

—the educational ISA (the system of the different public and private 'Schools'),

—the family ISA,

—the legal ISA,

—the political ISA (the political system, including the different Parties),

—the trade-union ISA,

—the communications ISA (press, radio and television, etc.),

—the cultural ISA (Literature, the Arts, sports, etc.) (143)

14. This disagreement finds Boxer even more strident in his disagreement with Squealer's propaganda. When the pigs decide to fire a gun to celebrate the repulsion of the men, Boxer expresses irritation:

'What is that gun firing for?' said Boxer.
'To celebrate our victory!' cried Squealer.
'What victory?' said Boxer. His knees were bleeding, he had lost a shoe and split his hoof, and a dozen pellets had lodged themselves in his hind leg.
'What victory, comrade? Have we not driven the enemy off our soil—the sacred soil of Animal Farm?'

'But they have destroyed the windmill. And we had worked on it for two years!'

'What matter? We will build another windmill. We will build six windmills if we feel like it. You do not appreciate, comrade, the mighty thing that we have done. The enemy was in occupation of this very ground that we stand upon. And now—thanks to the leadership of Comrade Napoleon—we have won every inch of it back again!'

'Then we have won back what we had before,' said Boxer.

'That is our victory,' said Squealer. (71)

15. V C. Letemendia's observation regarding how the animals' decency works against them is seen mostly strongly in Boxer:

> The diversity of the animal class, like the working class, is equally stressed by the differing personalities of the creatures. Just because all have been subjected to human rule, this does not mean that they will act as a united body once they take over the farm. The qualities which, for Orwell, clearly unite the majority of the animals with their human counterparts, the common working people, are a concern for freedom and equality in society and a form of 'innate decency' which prevents them from desiring power for any personal gain. While this decency hinders the worker animals from discovering the true nature of the pigs until the final scene, it also provides them with an instinctive feeling for what a fair society might actually look like. (16)

Letemendia's point highlights the mitigated nature of Orwell's optimism, as the author builds both decency and exploitation into the story, enabling the animals (and the reader) to see both the best and worst possible outcomes of the rebellion.

16. Orwell revels in such formulations, as one more example from his writing makes clear. Towards the end of *A Clergyman's Daughter*, Dorothy Hare, the protagonist, considers how she should continue acting as if she has faith even after having lost it. The answer is: "Beliefs change, thoughts change, but there is some inner part of the soul that does not change. Faith changes, but the need for faith remains the same as before" (292).

17. Valerie Meyers describes Orwell's mind in remarkably similar terms: "Orwell's paradoxical mind was capable of holding contrary views simultaneously. He often structures a piece of writing to oppose, balance and if possible reconcile opposites" (13).

PETER EDGERLY FIRCHOW

George Orwell's Dystopias:
From Animal Farm *to* Nineteen Eighty-Four

Happiness is notoriously difficult to describe, and pictures of a just and
well-ordered society are seldom either attractive or convincing.

George Orwell

Authentic Orwell

More than any other British writer of the first half of the twentieth century,
with the possible exception of the otherwise very different E. M. Forster,
George Orwell had an uncanny gift for quickly establishing a relationship
of trust with his readers. Encountering him, one has the feeling almost at
once that he is an intelligent, basically decent person who is being "straight"
with us, who is trying as honestly as he can to avoid mouthing the party
line, whether it's the party line of the Right, Left, or middle. At the same
time, he doesn't ostentatiously bare his chest or seek to occupy the lime-
light as the greatest sinner or truth teller of all or even just his own time.
Not only does he not metaphorically raise his own voice in his writing; he
despises others who raise theirs. Witness the contempt with which he treats
the fanatical Marxist sloganeer at the Left Book Club meeting in *Coming
Up for Air* (175ff.). Orwell's self-image of the quiet, diffident, fiercely independent commentator on politics and life in general is especially evident in
his essays—like Huxley and Forster, Orwell is one of the great essayists of

From *Modern Utopian Fictions: From H. G. Wells to Iris Murdoch*, pp. 97–129. © 2007 by the
Catholic University of America Press.

125

the period—as well as in his documentary books, *Down and Out in Paris and London*, *The Road to Wigan Pier*, and, most of all, *Homage to Catalonia*, which is about his participation in the Spanish Civil War.[1]

While his personality—his "persona," if you prefer—is a good part of the reason why we trust him, we also trust him because he is authentic. When one reads Orwell on the Spanish War, one knows that he's been there. One feels very differently too, I think, about reading a novel like *Animal Farm* or *Nineteen Eighty-Four* when one knows that the author has actually experienced what he is writing about. Not that George Orwell ever was an "animal"—though there undoubtedly is something very Orwellian about the skeptical donkey Benjamin in *Animal Farm*—or lived in the year 1984 (for him of course still thirty-five years into a future he never lived to see), but he had actually raised animals (as Alex Zwerdling says, the book "could only have been written by someone who had observed life on a farm and how animals behave very closely") and experienced life at the very bottom of the social ladder, as, among other things, a dishwasher in a Paris hotel and a hobo drifting through London and surroundings; and he had lived in some of the worst industrial slums of the black country during the most depressing years, as he did in Wigan. In very different circumstances, he had also experienced at first hand how brutally the Stalinist Communist Party operated in Spain, where he saw and felt how they fanatically tried to suppress and even "liquidate" him and his fellow anti-Franco fighters in the Trotskyist POUM (Partido Obrero de Unificación Marxista or "Workers' Party of Marxist Unification").[2]

In other words, George Orwell's books always rest on a solid foundation of lived experience. Though he is not afraid to generalize or criticize others from the perspective of that experience, he is never a mere windbag or "theoretician." When he notoriously censured W. H. Auden for justifying "necessary murders" during the Spanish War though Auden had never witnessed an actual murder himself, Orwell could point out that he, on the other hand, *had* experienced murder and not just killing (in Spain and probably in Burma too). By doing so he was claiming the authority of experience over mere theory. "So much of left-wing thought," he went on to generalize about what he took at the time to be martini-Marxists like Auden, "is a kind of playing with fire by people who don't even know that fire is hot" (1954, 243).

Interestingly, Orwell's experience exists on *both* sides. That is, not only was Orwell down and out in Paris and London, but he was also, as it were, up and inside in Rangoon and on the Irrawaddy. His first job—and the only one that he was ever fully trained to do, including his subsequent jobs as a journalist and novelist—was that of an officer in the Indian Colonial Constabulary in Burma, so that when he writes about O'Brien in *Nineteen Eighty-Four* or about Napoleon's specially trained dogs in *Animal Farm*, he is also writing in part from actual police experience. This is even true to some extent of Winston Smith's work at the Ministry of Truth. After all, it is probably not coincidental that Winston Smith's participation in the manufacture and re-manufacture of truth bears a resemblance to Orwell's wartime work in the propaganda section of the BBC. The two activities are not the same, of course, but they are close enough in a general way to count as real experience.

Orwell, in short, is an *authentic* writer whether he is describing the social depths or the social heights. (As a graduate of Eton College he also had personal experience of the uppermost segment of the upper classes in Britain.) That is why we trust him. And we trust him too because he is willing to admit to what might be thought of as flaws in his own character, as when in 1940, after expressing his readiness to kill Hitler if given the chance, he admits that he nevertheless can't help feeling a sneaking sympathy for him as an underdog. Then there is Orwell's notoriously sensitive nose, one that was able to ferret out stenches which he would go on to describe in lovingly nauseating detail, e.g., the odiferous chamber pot placed under the breakfast table in the disgusting lodgings he occupied while gathering the material that would eventually congeal into *The Road to Wigan Pier*. While we may not share Orwell's sympathy for the "underdog" Hitler or his olfactory obsessions and may even be put off a little by them, they definitely do serve to make him more "human."

Animal Farm as History and Dystopia

Among other things, *Animal Farm* is based on authentic farming experience. During the 1930s Orwell had tried his hand, admittedly not very successfully, at raising vegetables and even a select variety of small animals. Later, when he could afford to—ironically, partly as a result of the very good sales of *Animal Farm*—he lived for a time on a remote farm on the Scottish island of Jura, a farm that had no electricity and was accessible only on foot. It was something he had dreamed about doing for years. That dream is emblematic of the deep rift in Orwell's personality between downright, practical hands-on experience—his ingrained realism, if you like—and an idyllic, quite impractical nostalgia for a Romantic "golden" countryside such as never existed outside his imagination. His real nose may testify to the vile smells of his Wigan boarding house, but his visionary eye is always longing for the pristine bliss of an ideal Golden Country.

Though it would become hugely successful, *Animal Farm* was probably Orwell's most difficult book to get published. This despite the fact that Orwell was by then fairly well known as a sort of maverick left-wing writer of essays and reviews. Written in 1943–44, at a time when just about everybody else in England was enthusiastic about the Red Army's costly and unexpected success against Hitler's initially seemingly invincible army (and had already more or less forgotten about the Soviet Union's erstwhile alliance with Hitler and their joint invasion of Poland), *Animal Farm* was felt by the publishers to whom Orwell submitted the book to be the work of a traitor to the cause of social progress, rather like his friend Arthur Koestler's *Darkness at Noon*. Orwell, however, refused to be intimidated and continued to insist that he was a *socialist*, indeed far more of a socialist than those who were mouthing the Communist Party line and who were taking, as he put it in a telling phrase, "their cookery from Paris and their opinions from Moscow" (1954, 279). As he was also to remark later, in the Preface that he wrote for the Ukrainian translation of *Animal Farm*: "Indeed, in my opinion, nothing has contributed so much to the corruption of the original idea of Socialism as the belief that Russia is a Socialist country and that every act of its rulers must be excused, if not imitated" (1968b, 405).

Animal Farm was eventually accepted by a small, new publisher, Secker & Warburg, who brought it out in August 1945. In the United States it was rejected by eight publishers and did not actually appear until 1946 under the Harcourt, Brace & Company imprint. As all of this more or less concerted opposition suggests, *Animal Farm*, and of course Orwell too, were widely known to be potentially disruptive commodities, even though a few observers, such as the fellow-traveling Kingsley Martin, tried to dismiss them as merely trivial and ridiculous.[3] It was only after the collapse of the Soviet Union in 1989 that Orwell's status as a realistic commentator on the "socialism" of the Soviet Empire was fully vindicated.

Animal Farm, as virtually everyone realized who read the book at the time, either before or after it was published, and who reacted either positively or negatively to it, is intended to be read as a very close allegory of Soviet history from the time of the Revolution until about 1945 or at least until the Teheran Conference. In case, however, anyone still needs the allegory to be translated, here are the animal/historical equivalents:

Jones is the pre-1917 Russian ruling class. Manor Farm is tsarist Russia. Animal Farm is the Soviet Union. Old Major is a combination of Marx and Lenin.[4] Animalism is Marxism-Leninism. Snowball is Leon Trotsky. Napoleon is Josef Stalin. Squealer is Andrei Zdanov. Whymper is the generic capitalist intermediary, also representative of the so-called New Economic Policy of the 1920s. The pigs are the Communist Party membership. The domestic animals are the working class, especially the hard-working horses Boxer and Clover, with the sheep being the naive believers of all aspects of party doctrine. The wild animals are the rural peasantry, especially perhaps the kulaks, but possibly also the "Lumpenproletariat." (Even Old Major is unsure what to make of them.) The dogs trained by Napoleon are the NKVD (later the KGB). The humans are the bourgeoisie. Pilkington and Foxwood are Great Britain, and perhaps France too. Frederick and Pinchwood are Germany. Building the windmill is the electrification and industrialization of the Soviet Union. (According to a famous slogan attributed to Stalin, socialism plus electricity equals communism.) The Battle of the Cowshed is the defeat of the White Russians. The Battle of the Windmill is World War II. Moses the Raven is the Russian Orthodox Church, and his Sugarcandy Mountain is heaven. Mollie the vain horse represents those members of the working class who left the Soviet Union for opportunistic reasons. The hypocritical cat seems to have no specifically allegorical function. Benjamin the donkey is the novel's *raisonneur*, who expresses the outlook that comes closest to Orwell's own.[5]

Into the framework of this allegory Orwell places many, if not most, of the important historical and political events of the Soviet period, such as: (1) the expulsion of Trotsky by Stalin, along with the gradual "rectification" of the former's role in the Revolution—Trotsky, like both Snowball and, later, Emmanuel Goldstein in *Nineteen Eighty-Four*, is transformed into a traitor and universal scapegoat;[6] (2) the creation of a secret police loyal only to Stalin and his totalitarian regime; (3) the cunning but ultimately stupid and self-defeating "diplomacy" of Stalin in the 1930s, who thought he would be able to play off Great Britain and France against Germany; (4) the infamous show trials of the late thirties, with their trumped-up charges and confessions along with their summary executions; and (5) the gradual metamorphosis of the Communist Party from the "voice" of the people to the protective mask of a privileged caste, or, in Orwell's terms, the ultimate interchangeability of pigs and humans.[7]

More difficult to grasp than the political and historical allegory of *Animal Farm* is what the point of it all might be. That is, why didn't Orwell just tell us the "story" of how socialism was perverted in Stalin's Russia in straightforward and readily comprehensible terms? Why was it necessary for him to disguise that story in animal dress? And what are we to make of Orwell's rather odd claim in the subtitle that *Animal Farm* is a "fairy story"?

To these questions there are several possible answers.[8] To begin with, we need to remember that Orwell is writing fiction in *Animal Farm*, not history. Though the historical element is very strong in the novel—and indeed is essential to understanding what's going on in it—history has been coherently transposed into the very different and quite nonhistorical context of a fable, a context so far removed from the usual way history is written that, initially at least, readers are not aware that what they are reading is a peculiar retelling of Soviet history. It is precisely this unfamiliarity of context, and the gradual realization on the part of readers of what the book is really about, that causes them to see the historical events in a new light. Ironically, Orwell has succeeded in *Animal Farm* by using what has since come to be seen as a characteristically Soviet literary technique—"defamiliarization"—first described by the so-called Russian Formalists in the 1920s, to expose the crafty, underhanded maneuverings behind the Communist Party's accession to power.

This technique of defamiliarizing already familiar historical material and thereby making it "new" also has, literarily speaking, other interesting and positive side effects. For example, it helps to make the actions of the Party seem at times absurd and ridiculous, if not actually pathetic, as, for example, when, not long after the overthrow of Jones, under the leadership of the pigs the animals tour the farmhouse and find some hams hanging in the kitchen which they then proceed to take out for formal burial. So too with the account of Napoleon's supposedly imminent death after having, for the first time, sampled rather too much of old Jones's whisky. Furthermore, it allows Orwell to expose satirically the absurdity of the Stalinist cult of personality by having one hen remark to another: "Under the guidance of our Leader, Comrade Napoleon, I have laid five eggs in six days" (67). Also the "fairy" tale designation of the story serves to defamiliarize our response, since it implies that the historical allegory is really part of some incredible "fairy" tale that no adult person would ever accept as real or even realistic.[9] The strong implication is that most histories of the Soviet Union up to this point have been "fairy tales."

Even more interesting and probably significant, however, are the implications of transposing a story that is fundamentally social (i.e., the story of the development of the Soviet Union) into a primarily biological or essentialist framework. The story then becomes one of nature rather than nurture, of the essential "animal condition," as seen especially from the donkey Benjamin's point of view. If such a reading of the book holds up, then it would seem that Orwell is presenting here a critique of the Soviet Union from what looks like a conservative point of view. That is, he is apparently arguing that basic human (or, rather, "animal") nature is such that, no matter what the political system might be, the "pigs" will inevitably rise to the top. The lesson then would be that those creatures who are the greediest, least scrupulous, and most power-hungry, regardless of whether they are human or animal, are the ones who will rule, no matter what the current official political doctrine or theory is. What takes place at the Animal Farm, then, or in the Soviet Union, for that matter, is less an example of Marxist dialectical materialism and more a version of Vilfredo Pareto's notorious "circulation of the elites." Instead of elite humans, we are here confronted with elite pigs—not a big difference, as it turns out. *Plus ça change*, as it were, *plus ça reste la même chose*.[10]

Is Orwell implying something like this? Yes, I think he is. Toward the end of his life he did, after all, become a kind of Tory anarchist—as he once described himself (Crick 1980, 174)—or even Tory socialist, someone, that is, who, though without exercising doublethink, managed to fuse conservative ideas (about patriotism, for example) with radical ones (about the equitable distribution of wealth, for example).[11] Not that reading *Animal Farm* in essentialist terms really represents a radical deviation from the socialist perspective. In orthodox Marxist doctrine there is, after all, a fundamental assumption about human "economic" nature that resembles the one that Orwell appears to be making in *Animal Farm*, namely, that those who own the means of production are also those who exercise the power in any society. And hidden behind this assumption is yet another assumption that it takes a certain kind of creature to secure the ownership of those means of production in the first place. (This second, more or less invisible assumption goes back to Hegel's theory about the origin and development of the master/slave dichotomy. Marx, as the usual cliché has it, notoriously turned Hegel on his head.) In *Animal Farm*, though Napoleon and the pigs may not "own" the means of production in the technical sense of possessing a legal piece of paper that says they do—though at the end of the story there is in fact such a piece of paper—the pigs behave as if they own the farm and have a canine police force to back up their claim. Furthermore, there is the fact that, from the reader's point of view, it is Benjamin (and not, as Boxer maintains, Napoleon) who is proved "always right." This too would seem to support the essentialist position. Finally, there is a connection here to James Burnham's argument in *The Managerial Revolution*—a book from which Orwell borrowed several important ideas and which he admired, though with many reservations—that the real power in all contemporary societies (whether socialist, fascist, or capitalist) is vested in the managerial class. The pigs, therefore, will always behave like pigs, which in effect means that a pig will always be Pig Brother.

Choosing the genre of the fable for his retelling of the Soviet experiment had the additional advantage that it allowed Orwell more readily to present his material in the form of a satire than would have been the case if he had written it up as straightforward history. The continuing juxtaposition of the initially ideal seven commandments (and their continuing downward revision) with the reality of the pigs' behavior constitutes one of the most effective means of showing what sort of dystopia the farm of the animals is turning into. It provides an easily comprehensible—for most readers if not for most animals—frame of reference by which to gauge the moral deterioration of the revolution and its eventual collapse into a moral pigsty. The initial hopes for the establishment of a utopia, as promised both in Old Major's "I have a dream" speech and in the singing of "Beasts of England," are dashed as the pigs progressively pervert or subvert the "principles of Animalism" on which the Animal Farm had been based.[12] The utopian "golden future time" which the song foretells grows increasingly gray and drab—not to say "leaden"—despite the claims made by Squealer when, at the behest of "Comrade" Napoleon, he announces that "Beasts of England" is no longer to be sung. The reason? Because in the song the animals had "expressed our longing for a better society in the days to come. But that society has now been established. Clearly this song has no longer any purpose" (62).[13]

Are we therefore to read *Animal Farm* primarily as a satire on the folly of trying to establish a fair and equitable society in which workers would be treated justly? Is the dream of a "golden future time" a pipe dream pure and simple? Are the conclusions to be drawn from the attempt to establish an animal farm entirely pessimistic? Is the sardonic Benjamin the only animal who is, in the final analysis, always right?

There is certainly a large body of evidence to support this sort of negative view of the story. The pessimism is especially evident in the recurrent preoccupation of the animals (and the narrator) with determining whether the farm is better off under animal (or, rather, porcine) management than it was under Jones's. More and more, as Napoleon's policies take effect, the implication seems to be that the farm is worse off. Initially, despite a variety of hardships and setbacks, the animals had at least managed to get as much food (though no more) as they did in Jones's day. This is because, while they may be working longer hours, their work has become more efficient; and since "no animal now stole," certain kinds of jobs, such as maintaining fences and hedges, were now unnecessary (46).[14] And, of course, the farm now "belongs" to the animals, and, what is even more important, no animals are being slaughtered.

This difficult but still tolerable and even hopeful situation on the farm changes radically for the worse when, at Napoleon's command, a number of animals are killed by his dogs after confessing to a secret collaboration with Snowball. At the end of these "show trials" and summary executions, the air becomes "heavy with the smell of blood, which had been unknown there since the expulsion of Jones." Though these killings are no more numerous than they had been under Jones, they are perceived to be "far worse" because they are carried out by the animals themselves on the orders of other animals (61). Whatever else may or may not be true about these killings, there can be no question that a moral deterioration has set in.

This is confirmed when it becomes apparent that, although the farm itself eventually becomes richer and more prosperous, the animals themselves are no better off "except of course for the pigs and dogs" (92). The remaining animals seem to work harder and get less food than before, though even the older ones are increasingly unable to remember if even "in the early days of the rebellion ... things had been better or worse than now." They can't tell because there is no reliable measure by which they can compare their present condition with their former one; there are only "Squealer's lists, which invariably demonstrated that everything was getting better and better" (93).[15] Only Benjamin, whose memory seems to work more reliably, claims that in his experience there is not much difference between conditions prevailing now and then—"hunger, hardship, and disappointment being, so he said, the unalterable law of life" (93). But even Benjamin may occasionally be wrong. When, at the very end of the novel, Mr. Pilkington and some other farmers visit the farm, they conclude with some satisfaction that "the lower animals on Animal Farm did more work and received less food than any animals in the county" (98).

So the experiment of the animals taking over and running their own farm is to be judged a failure? Yes, apparently so, though neither Orwell nor his narrator takes much joy in arriving at such a conclusion. If the evidence clearly shows that in practice the farm is no better off, as far as most of the animals are concerned, than it was before the expulsion of Jones, still in theory that expulsion retains a great part of its justification. In other words, the final message seems to be that however much the reality may disappoint us, we should nevertheless adhere to the ideal. For this reason *Animal Farm* should not be read merely as a satire. Or, put another way, its satirical parts are so bitter precisely because the ideal is still believed in. The lies and cruelty of Napoleon, and the boundless chutzpah of his apologist Squealer in justifying every violation of the original seven commandments, are a gross perversion of old Major's dream of universal animal equality and happiness. Orwell's task, as he saw it, was to expose that chutzpah, that perversion, not to question the original dream. After all, if those original commandments were not the potential basis for a good society, why bother to expose their violation? In the end, then, *Animal Farm* affirms the dream of a "golden future time," while at the same time denying that such a golden future time has yet arrived. It also shows that, no matter how disappointing the outcome, there once had been at least a glimpse of what such a time might be like during the days immediately following the rebellion and the takeover of Manor Farm by the animals.

In 1943, at more or less the same moment when he was starting work on *Animal Farm*, Orwell put down some reflections on how the working class could never accommodate itself to fascism. These reflections are also relevant to how we should respond to the failure of the socialist experiment in *Animal Farm*. "The struggle of the working class," Orwell tells us in his essay on "Looking Back on the Spanish War," "is like the growth of a plant. The plant is blind and stupid, but it knows enough to keep pushing upwards towards the light, and it will do this in the face of endless discouragements. What are the workers struggling for? Simply for the decent life which they are more and more aware is now technically possible." Not that the working-class "plant" always succeeds in getting what it wants, any more than the working-class "animals" do. But there are occasions when it does happen, even if only briefly. One such occasion, according to Orwell, was the period just at the beginning of the war in Spain, when "for a while, people were acting consciously, moving towards a goal which they wanted to reach and believed they could reach. It accounted for the curiously buoyant feeling that life in Government Spain had during the early months of the war. The common people knew in their bones that the Republic was their friend and Franco was their enemy" (1954, 208). What are we to conclude from these reflections? I think we are meant to conclude that there is and always will be hope; and that this hope resides principally, as Winston Smith will put it in Orwell's next novel, in the "proles," that is, in the human and animal embodiments of what is best in the working class, such as the Italian antifascist soldier whom Orwell met at the beginning of his stay in Barcelona (and about whom he later wrote one of his rare poems), or, for that matter, in such animals as the rather stupid but nonetheless noble and admirable Boxer in *Animal Farm*.

The End of Oceania

Nineteen Eighty-Four has a distinguished and variegated literary ancestry.[16] To begin with, there is Evgenij Zamiatin's *We*, which Orwell had read with admiration in 1944 on the recommendation of Gleb Struve.[17] Then there is his friend Arthur Koestler's *Darkness at Noon*, and behind Koestler, Dostoevsky's *The Possessed*, both of which helped to shape the debate between O'Brien and Winston Smith in the last part of Orwell's novel. Also, and rather more obviously, there is Aldous Huxley's *Brave New World*, which Orwell may be said to stand on its head, replacing Our Freud's sex drive with Big Brother's lust for power.

There is at least one scene in Orwell's novel which directly recalls Huxley's, namely, when Julia and Winston are just about to make love for the first time: "She stood looking at him for an instant, then felt at the zipper of her overalls. And yes! It was almost as in his dream. Almost as swiftly as he had imagined it, she had torn her clothes off, and when she flung them aside it was with that same magnificent gesture by which a whole civilization seemed to be annihilated" (110). In *Brave New World*, it is Lenina who disrobes before John Savage: "Zip! Zip! . . . She stepped out of her bell-bottomed trousers. Her zippicamicknicks were a pale shell pink . . . Zip! The rounded pinkness fell apart like a neatly divided apple. . . . Still wearing her shoes and socks, and her rakishly tilted round white cap she advanced towards him" (193). Unlike John, however, who interprets Lenina's behavior (quite rightly) as evidence of her promiscuity and proceeds to revile her, Winston delights in the evidence of Julia's sexual experience. "The more men you've had," he tells her, "the more I love you. . . . I hate purity, I hate goodness. I don't want any virtue to exist anywhere. I want everyone to be corrupt to the bones" (111).

Here the influence of *Brave New World* is at one and the same time acknowledged and rejected. For Orwell, at this point in the novel at any rate, it is the sex drive that is the most dangerous enemy of the power drive.[18] That, no doubt, is also why, as O'Brien tells Winston later, Oceania's neurologists are busily at work on ways to abolish the orgasm. (This is an idea that would be utterly abhorrent to O'Brien's counterpart in *Brave New World*, the gentle World Controller, Mustapha Mond.) It may also be why for Winston the embodiment of his persistent hope in the "proles" is the massive figure of the woman whom he hears singing and whom he also sees from the window of his love nest above Charrington's junk shop. She has hips at least a meter across, as Julia disparagingly points out, and possesses practically no mind, but Winston finds her beautiful nevertheless. She has "strong arms, a warm heart, and a fertile belly," so fertile indeed that Winston speculates she may have given birth to as many as fifteen children. Where O'Brien destroys, in other and somewhat hopeful words, she creates. In Winston's mind, she represents the "hundreds or thousands of millions of people just like this, people ignorant of one another's existence, held apart by walls of hatred and lies, and yet almost exactly the same—people who had never learned to think but were storing up in their hearts and bellies and muscles the power that would one day overturn the world. . . . The future belonged to the proles. . . . The proles were immortal. You could not doubt it when you looked at that valiant figure in the yard. In the end their awakening would come" (195–96). Significantly, in *Brave New World* John Savage shares, for a time at least, a similar hope that the lower-caste workers will rise up and destroy the New World State—a hope that turns out to be just as deluded as Winston's.

Small wonder, then, that Orwell should have sent Huxley a copy of his new book immediately after its publication, and was anxious to know what Huxley's verdict would be.[19]

And, of course, there is also the influence of *Animal Farm*. Both novels share a preoccupation with the Soviet Union's betrayal of the ideals (as Orwell saw them) of socialism. Both feature prominently the transformation of Trotsky into a scapegoat for all the inadequacies of the Soviet system, though in *Nineteen Eighty-Four* the Trotsky figure, Emmanuel Goldstein, is provided with some (apparently fictitious) opportunity to justify himself by means of "The Book," something Snowball was not able to do in *Animal Farm*. Both novels make much of the massive personality cult devoted to Stalin, with the glaring, larger-than-life depictions of the heavily moustachioed face of Big Brother being virtually omnipresent in Oceania.[20] Both books devote a good deal of attention to the ways in which the Party brainwashes its adherents (e.g., notably the sheep in *Animal Farm* and the bumbling, brainwashed Parsons in *Nineteen Eighty-Four*), as well as to the disproportionate and utterly irrational punishments meted out to alleged traitors and saboteurs. Both books are also centrally concerned with the inability of the working class—though in *Nineteen Eighty-Four*, it's primarily the Outer Party—to gauge whether the postrevolutionary society is better off than the prerevolutionary one. This preoccupation also extends beyond practical concerns to a larger, metaphysical worry about how totalitarian states are able to reshape the past for their own purposes, thereby controlling the identity not only of their societies but also of their individual citizens.

There are also important differences between the two books. Most obviously, there is in *Animal Farm* no protagonist like Winston Smith, no love affair with someone like Julia, and no talkative torturer like O'Brien. There is also no distinction between the Inner and Outer Parties, no vast population of working-class people (representing 85 percent of the total population) who are left more or less undisturbed by the Party, which subjects them only to occasional outbursts of propaganda and designates for liquidation only the most obvious potential proletarian rebels. There is also the important difference that Oceania is characterized by continuous war, with enemy prisoners being reviled and sometimes executed, and with (enemy?) rockets regularly exploding and killing people. In *Animal Farm*, while war may be a continual danger—at least until the pigs become fully "human"—there are only two actual interludes of warfare: the Battle of the Cowshed and the Battle of the Windmill.

The most important difference may actually be that *Animal Farm* is about the past (as well as a little about the present), whereas *Nineteen Eighty-Four* is entirely about the future. *Animal Farm* ends more or less with the consolidation of power by the pigs following the Battle of the Windmill, that is, translated into historical terms, with the end of World War II in 1945—also the year when the novel was published. *Nineteen Eighty-Four*, on the other hand, differs radically in that it imagines a future based on the tendencies of the present. Completed in 1948, *Nineteen Eighty-Four* simply reverses the last two digits of that year, unmistakably indicating thereby that it is a book about what the present will likely turn into in the not too distant future. *Animal Farm* ends with pigs and humans becoming indistinguishable, an idea which, though bitterly ironic, can still raise a smile; not so, however, *Nineteen Eighty-Four*, which leaves the reader with little to laugh or even smile about. Pig Brother, swinish though he may be, still isn't Big Brother. Paradoxically, Pig Brother is still "human"; he is selfish, egotistical, vain, full of foibles like getting drunk or hogging the milk and apples. He is even cruel and conniving, like Jones, but he is not a monster.

That is not the case, however, with Big Brother or with his principal representative in *Nineteen Eighty-Four*, O'Brien. The most remarkable thing about O'Brien is that, in the ordinary way, he seems to have no vices at all. Though he is not an "animal," he definitely isn't "human." So far as we can tell, he devotes just about all of his time to discovering, manipulating, "curing," and eliminating social deviants like Winston Smith. Judging from the minute detail that he seems to have accumulated over the previous seven years about Winston's life and mind, along with the elaborate premeditated malice with which he responds to Winston's allegedly errant ways, he must be putting in nearly twenty-four-hour days at the Ministry of Love (with additional, briefer interludes at the Ministry of Truth). No wonder Winston Smith thinks O'Brien looks tired.[21]

If O'Brien is typical of the elite of the inner Party—and it's clear we are meant to think so, just as we are meant to think of Winston Smith as typical of the Outer Party—then it's hard to escape the conclusion that already by 1984 human/porcine nature has changed dramatically, at least so far as the Inner Party is concerned. Most obviously, it has become monomaniacally focused on one thing only: POWER. Unlike, say, *Brave New World*, it is a power deliberately based on hatred rather than on love. Nothing else matters, as O'Brien explains to Winston, and in the future beyond 1984, nothing else will matter, if possible, even less:

> The old civilizations claimed that they were founded on love and justice. Ours is founded upon hatred. In our world there will be no emotions except fear, rage, triumph, and self-abasement. Everything else we shall destroy—everything. Already we are breaking down the habits of thought which have survived from before the Revolution.... Children will be taken from their mothers as one takes eggs from a hen. The sex instinct will be eradicated. Procreation will be an annual formality like the renewal of a ration card. We shall abolish the orgasm.... All competing pleasures will be destroyed. But always—do not forget this, Winston—there will be the intoxication of power, constantly increasing and constantly growing subtler. Always, at every moment, there will be the thrill of victory, the sensation of trampling on an enemy who is helpless. If you want a picture of the future, imagine a boot stamping on a human face—forever. (238–39)

Though admittedly one should be careful about reaching definitive conclusions before all the evidence is in, still, after the momentous events of 1989, it definitely looks like O'Brien's insane predictions have not proved particularly accurate.[22] No doubt, the boot on the human face is still stamping away busily in various parts of the world, including places that are fairly close to home—and such sadistic stamping may even continue "forever" into the future—but it unquestionably is not the exclusive "intoxication" in the post-1984 world that O'Brien thought it would become. On the contrary, as Francis Fukuyama has famously observed, the currently triumphant consumerist society, with its videos, burgers, drugs, and sexually "pneumatic" delights, looks far more likely to be the final form of the future for most of us living in the West (i.e., in "Oceania"), if, that is, it has not already turned into our present.[23] These days, no matter what one may think of our devotion to consumerism, one can still say that, comparatively speaking, it is fortunate that O'Brien—or whatever other name an equivalent contemporary sadist might be operating under—is more likely to be found playing some virtual-reality chainsaw video game than conducting electric shock sessions in Room 101. The idea that eliminating all pleasures, except the unique "pleasure" of stamping with one's boot on some hapless face, would satisfy an intelligent person "forever" is, in retrospect (but not only in retrospect), absurd. On the surface, at least, such single-minded focus on just one "pleasure" seems self-defeating even in O'Brien's own terms, since the elimination of other ways of enjoying power, such as, say, depriving people of sexual pleasure, is unlikely to make the "intoxication of power" grow "subtler." Cruder is what it would make it grow, even boring, like reading the Marquis de Sade's *120 Days of Sodom*. For most people, it seems fair to conclude, even the vicarious experience of a couple of days in Sodom is more than enough. And de Sade, though no doubt quite as mad as O'Brien, at least had enough sense to retain the orgasm.

O'Brien is actually a far better and more realistic metaphysician than he is a prophet or moralist.[24] His insistence that the nature of reality is internal rather than external, that it can be solely determined by the Party, represents an interesting revision of the famous verdict of heresy by the Church regarding Galileo's contention that the earth revolved around the sun.[25] Though, like Galileo, Winston initially reacts with the equivalent of the former's whispered "eppur se muove" ("nevertheless it [the earth] moves"), he is finally persuaded that 2 + 2 actually make 5, and that, if he so wished, O'Brien could levitate. In the end Winston is even persuaded to love Big Brother, something the Church was never able to make Galileo do with the pope.

Party reality, in other words, is a kind of "bottled" reality, very much as in *Brave New World*, though the "reality" contained in the bottles is, in each case, very different. And, as in Huxley's novel, where the Alphas enjoy a certain freedom not to be infantile (that is, they are able, when absolutely necessary, to emerge from the "bottles" of their conditioning), members of the Inner Party also have access, at least to the extent permitted by "doublethink," to an "unbottled" reality.[26] This is notably proved by O'Brien's possession of the supposedly destroyed photograph of the discredited former inner Party members, Rutherford, Aronson, and Jones. Somewhere, then, in the Ministry of Truth, there must be a separate set of files preserving an unrevised record of actual historical events. Big Brother, so it would appear, endorses not only doublethink but also double-entry bookkeeping.[27]

In this connection, it is probably significant that Newspeak, at least on the evidence of Orwell's novel, is never spoken—not by the proles, not by members of the Outer Party, and not even by members of the Inner Party. While the Appendix on Newspeak does explicitly address the issue of how the language is to be spoken in the future (in a "gabbling style ... at once staccato and monotonous" [275]), it provides no convincing examples of such speech, and, in any event, the Appendix is not really relevant for reasons that will become apparent a little later in this chapter. The reality that Newspeak is designed to "bottle" is, so far as Winston and his contemporaries are concerned, strictly a written reality. All spoken language continues to be entirely in "Oldspeak," which means that forbidden thoughts can still be expressed so long as they are expressed orally. In that sense, "Newspeak" is a misnomer; it should really be called "Newwrite."[28]

Given O'Brien's stated predilection for the supposedly ever subtler "intoxications of power," it seems, initially at least, rather puzzling why O'Brien should be devoting so much time and effort in the reformation of Winston Smith's character by means of a variety of rather crude methods of torture. Though Winston is not stupid, his life so far has not been in any way unusual or distinguished. While he evidently possesses a certain gift for rewriting snippets of history, especially as contained in old newspapers, and even produces occasional quasi-Newspeak articles for the *Times*, he is otherwise quite as nondescript as his surname suggests he must be. What's more, as he tells Julia at the first opportunity, he is thirty-nine years old, has a wife he can't get rid of, suffers from varicose veins, and has false teeth. Small wonder that he can't quite grasp what she sees in him. For that matter, it's hard to grasp what O'Brien sees in him either.

One explanation for O'Brien's concentrated interest in Winston might be that he thinks of Winston as a kind of "Everyman," which would at least account for Winston's ordinariness. An everyman, after all, has to be ordinary if he is to qualify as an everyman. Still, Winston's ordinariness does not help explain why Julia should be attracted to him. Her reason—that she "saw something" potentially rebellious in his face (108)—seems rather lame and even unlikely, since, if Winston is good at anything, he's good at maintaining the "ordinary" orthodox poker face required to escape the attentions of the omnipresent telescreens.[29] Perhaps the real reason for Julia's otherwise inexplicable attraction to Winston is to be found in Orwell's own private preconceptions about women, whom in actual life he usually considered undersexed and even frigid. Julia, in other words, is a kind of wish fulfillment, for Orwell as well as for Winston. As for Winston's ordinariness, the primary reason for that, other than camouflage, may be to allow the reader to identify with someone who is "ordinary" in much the same way most readers are. In this way readers can be made to feel (even "bellyfeel," as the Newspeak word has it) what it's like to live in the Oceania of 1984. Otherwise the novel might easily have degenerated into a mere treatise along the lines of Emmanuel Goldstein's "Book," only longer. As it is, *Nineteen Eighty-Four* already bears a heavy burden of discursiveness, not only in the assigned readings in "The Book" but also in the discussions between O'Brien and Winston that take up much of the last part of the novel. For this reason we should perhaps be grateful that Julia is only a revolutionary from the waist down, someone who barely manages to keep awake when Winston starts reading out loud from "The Book."

The most compelling explanation for O'Brien's curiously intense interest in Winston, however, is to be found in O'Brien's own explicit assertion and prediction that "this drama that I have played out with you during seven years will be played out over and over again, generation after generation. Always in subtler forms" (239). Here O'Brien acknowledges that he has been systematically manipulating Winston's physical and mental life since 1977. In ways that ironically resemble Winston's revising and even inventing historical and biographical facts, O'Brien has apparently spent much of his time during the last seven years totally reinventing Winston's life and mind. This persistent and massive interference with and involvement in Winston's behavior and thinking (even dreaming) is apparent only when one goes back and looks more closely at earlier scenes in the book that now assume additional significance. Then one suddenly realizes that *Nineteen Eighty-Four* is really a book with two plots: an overt and a covert one. So, for example, the fact that Winston's room possesses a nook where he can hide from the telescreen seems fortuitous until we recognize that this too was part of O'Brien's plan to lull Winston into a false sense of security. Months later, languishing in the cellars of the Ministry of Truth, Winston himself realizes that "for seven years the Thought Police had watched him like a beetle under a magnifying glass. There was no physical act, no word spoken aloud, that they had not noticed, no train of thought that they had not been able to infer. Even the speck of whitish dust on the cover of his diary they had carefully replaced" (247). There seems to be no length to which O'Brien is not prepared to go, no expense that he is not willing to incur, in order to entrap Winston. The "junk shop" with its "owner," the elaborately disguised Thought Police official Charrington, has been set up and kept in readiness for years—Potemkin Village-style—apparently just in order to deceive Winston. The effort and the planning that must have gone into these stage props stagger the imagination.

Winston's dream seven years earlier—and the association of that dream with the as yet unfamiliar face of O'Brien—that they will meet "in the room where there is no darkness," seems at first promising (the absence of darkness suggests hope) and only in retrospect becomes ominous (22, 91). His detailed envisioning of the "Golden Country" even before he goes there to meet Julia for the first time may strike the reader as odd, but it only becomes suspicious on rereading. Then it becomes clear that somehow either Julia herself must have been complicit with O'Brien from the beginning or else she too has been manipulated by him in much the same way as Winston has been. How else to explain the proleptic vision Winston has of a "girl with dark hair coming toward him across the field" who overwhelms him with "admiration for the gesture with which she had thrown her clothes aside. With its grace and carelessness it seemed to annihilate a whole culture, a whole system of thought . . ." (27). At this point Winston has not even met Julia. Later, when they do meet in the Golden Country and Winston sees Julia act out in reality what he had earlier dreamed she would do, he says to himself, " . . . yes! It was almost as in his dream. Almost as swiftly . . . she flung [her clothes] aside . . . with that same magnificent gesture by which a whole civilization seemed to be annihilated" (110).[30]

Once we as readers become aware of the extent of the covert plot of the novel, we are inevitably led to wonder what the point of it might be. The most obvious answer to this question is, once again, provided by O'Brien, at least implicitly. His extraordinary manipulation of Winston is both proof of his immense, almost godlike power and also proof of its "subtlety." The more obvious and therefore cruder expressions of his power only follow later, in the beatings and in the electroshock treatments carried out in Room 101. The boot in the face, in other words, is only the culmination, as it were, of the stab in the back, or, more accurately, of the twist of the mind.

So O'Brien's "intoxication of power" is subtle after all? On the evidence of Winston's experience, yes, it would seem to be. But what about O'Brien's claim that Winston's experience is a mere preliminary to the drama that "will be played out over and over again, generation after generation, always in subtler forms?" This claim seems to border on madness and may be intended to be read as an example of O'Brien's hubris. After all, if the sex impulse and even the orgasm are to be abolished in the future, the possible areas for "subtle" expressions of power will be drastically diminished rather than increased. If there's no interest in sex, there obviously can be no future equivalent of the Winston/Julia relationship; and if, as O'Brien claims, the parent/

child bond will also be destroyed, there can be no guilt feelings of the sort that Winston repeatedly feels about being responsible for the death of his mother and younger sister. There is the further complication that the future refinements in Newspeak will increasingly prohibit the expression—and ultimately even the conception—of subtlety. The point of Newspeak, after all, is to eliminate complexity and subtlety, not to foster them. What then will be the future sources of the supposedly ever more subtle playing out of the drama of power? Is it to be always the boot in the face? Forever? Unless he is utterly mad, this must seem an unattractive prospect even for O'Brien. That it apparently does not strike him as unattractive inevitably raises suspicions that he is utterly mad and that his madness will have "subtle" and rather drastic consequences.[31] Readers of *Nineteen Eighty-Four* should be careful, as William Steinhoff points out, not to confuse O'Brien's views on these matters with Orwell's. He "did not believe that Machiavelli, Burnham, and O'Brien were right. He did not believe that 'sadistic power-hunger' is the ultimate motive for human conduct" (1975, 203–4).

These suspicions are confirmed in the Appendix on "The Principles of Newspeak." Unlike Goldstein's "Book," there is no indication that this Appendix has been fabricated by O'Brien and/or other members of the Inner Party in order to mislead people like Winston. We can therefore accept it as a "genuine" description of the status of Newspeak and, by implication at least, of the status of the society that has developed it. We can infer that the Appendix seems to have been written sometime after 1984, "when Oldspeak was still the normal means of communication" (277), and 2050, the date for which "the final adoption of Newspeak had been fixed" (279). The opening sentence of the Appendix reads as follows: "Newspeak was the official language of Oceania and had been devised to meet the ideological needs of Ingsoc, or English Socialism."

There are several odd things about this sentence. To begin with, it's odd that any likely Oceanic reader of the Appendix would need to be told that Ingsoc means "English Socialism." Indeed, it's unlikely that such a reader would even understand what the reference to "English" means, since, according to the novel, England no longer exists but has long ago been replaced by an "Airstrip One" that is part of a larger international conglomerate named Oceania. Even odder is the statement that "Newspeak was the language of Oceania." If it was the language of Oceania, what is the language of Oceania now? Apparently, it's English, for that is the language in which the Appendix is written. But if English still is the language of Oceania, even long after 1984, and if the meaning of Ingsoc still needs to be explained at a time when the development of Newspeak was scheduled to be completed, then the kind of society described in *Nineteen Eighty-Four* either no longer exists or has changed beyond recognition. From all these peculiarities it appears that the Appendix, very much like the novel that precedes it, has both an overt and a covert meaning.

It could of course be argued that the fact that the Appendix is written in the past tense constitutes no proof that Oceania is no longer functioning as described in the novel. The novel itself, after all, is written in the past tense. To this objection, one can raise the counterobjection that the Appendix is not part of the novel but is clearly designated as an "appendix"; in other words it is something that follows the principal part of the book and presumably helps to clarify it or some part of it. Significantly, its form is not narrative but discursive. The Appendix therefore could and probably should have been written in the present tense, the tense in which most descriptive essays (e.g., like this one) are written. That it wasn't suggests Orwell had an ulterior motive in not doing so. This hypothesis may become more convincing when it is apparent that there is nothing grammatically or idiomatically wrong with changing the opening sentence into the present tense: "Newspeak is the language of Oceania and has been devised to meet the ideological needs of Ingsoc."

Even so, there is an additional problem even after the sentence has been transposed into the present, because it is still written in English, not in Newspeak. However, that objection can be discounted by noting that no contemporary reader of *Nineteen Eighty-Four*, either now or in 1949, would be able, or would have been able, to make out the meaning of so complex a document as the Appendix if it had been written in Newspeak, even supposing that Orwell had had the ability or desire to write it in that "language." (He could, of course, have used "cablese," which would have been comprehensible to most journalists at least.) Besides, there is the further objection that Newspeak was designed to eliminate the possibility of writing complex documents like this one.[32]

All in all, then, there seems to be a good deal of evidence to support the conclusion that we are meant to read the Appendix as conveying a double meaning, much as the novel itself does. Assuming, however, that this conclusion is indeed valid, there then follows another, perhaps even more momentous problem that needs to be addressed, namely, what was it that brought Ingsoc and the Party down? Was it, as Winston hoped and even predicted, the proles?[33] Are we to conclude that the "beautiful" working-class woman with her fertile meter-wide hips was too formidable an adversary for O'Brien after all? Or was it Goldstein's Brotherhood that, despite O'Brien's boastful claims, was not mythical after all, but in fact finally managed to infiltrate the Inner Party and destroy it?

There is and can be no definitive answer to these questions, or at least no direct answer. Indirectly, however, one can surmise that it was O'Brien himself (and his fellow Inner Party members) who brought down the prevailing system. The evidence for this conclusion is contained in O'Brien's own words and behavior. His peculiar predictions about the abolition of the orgasm and even of the sex drive as such, his ravings about the "ever subtler" intoxications of power when it is obvious that those "intoxications" could only become ever cruder and more boring, suggest that O'Brien, intelligent and hard-working though he is, is also utterly mad. But if this is so, there is no escaping the conclusion that no stable state can be built on the speculations of a madman. If nothing else, in 1948 the drastic and horrifying results wrought by the power-intoxicated and utterly mad Adolf Hitler were as yet staring everyone in Europe in the face. Hitler's thousand-year *Reich* lasted exactly twelve years. O'Brien's "forever" may last a little longer. But in the end, while O'Brien is able to convince Winston that $2 + 2 = 5$, and while he is even able to abolish history when he wants to, he nevertheless cannot control the future or abolish it.[34] Instead, the future will abolish him. Despite his grandiose and overweening claims, there are limits to O'Brien's power, as well as to the power of an institutionalized Ingsoc. The last and greatest of the many ironies of *Nineteen Eighty-Four*, then, is that the hope for the overthrow of Oceania resides neither in the proles nor in Emmanuel Goldstein's Trotskyists. The hope is in O'Brien.[35]

NOTES

1. For more on Orwell's success in establishing his "persona," see Firchow (1992).

2. Orwell may have partly modeled the Thought Police in *Nineteen Eighty-Four* on memories of being observed by Stalinist police in Barcelona at the end of his stay there. What he probably did not know, however, is that the British Secret Service (MI5) had been keeping tabs on him as far back as 1936, primarily because they (somewhat obtusely) suspected him of being a Communist. The Wigan police report to MI5 opined that "it would appear from his mode of living that he is an author, or has some connection with literary work, as he devotes most of his time to writing" (Travis 2005).

3. Shortly before his death Orwell provided the Foreign Office's Information Research Department (a semi-secret propaganda agency) with a list of people he suspected of being "crypto-communists." He intended the list to be used in preventing the IRD from hiring the wrong people for its work. Among the names is that of Kingsley Martin, described by Orwell as "too dishonest to be outright 'crypto', or fellow traveller, but reliably pro-Russian on all major issues" (Ash 2003). Such lists seem to have been a kind of habit with Orwell. According to Stephen Spender, Orwell had expressed his willingness to "draw up a list of intellectuals who would be willing to collaborate with the Nazis if they succeeded in invading England" (Steinhoff 1975, 221).

4. More Marx than Lenin probably, given Orwell's view, expressed in 1945, that "one ought, I believe, to admit that all the seeds of evil were there from the start

and that things would not have been substantially different if Lenin or Trotsky had remained in control" (1968a, 18). Since Old Major dies before the uprising of the animals, it would seem more likely that he is to be identified with Marx than Lenin. Otto Friedrich, however, claims that Old Major is Lenin, whereas Bernard Crick states with equal certainty that Old Major is Marx and that Lenin "does not figure in the story" (Friedrich 1994, 92; Crick 1989, 172).

5. According to Robert Lee, Benjamin "is essentially selfish, representing a view of human nature that is apolitical, and thus can hardly be, as some readers hold, the spokesman for Orwell within the book" (1986, 50).

6. Orwell's use of a Trotsky figure as the scapegoat in both *Animal Farm* and *Nineteen Eighty-Four* has its obvious historical origin in the treatment of Trotsky and Trotskyists after the expulsion (and "expunging") of Trotsky by Stalin, but there are also personal reasons for Orwell's intense, almost obsessive concern with the fate of Trotsky and his followers. This obsession is probably traceable to Orwell's being hounded out of Barcelona (and nearly killed there) for supposedly being a "Trotsky-ist" (Shelden 1991, 270).

7. An overly literal reading of *Animal Farm*, however, as in the case of Northrop Frye, can lead to absurd conclusions, such as that the end of the story affirms the reinstitution of the tsar (1986, 10).

8. According to C. M. Woodhouse's somewhat murky analysis, Orwell uses the fairy story to further his purpose of writing a story set "in a world beyond good and evil," one which when transcribed "into terms of highly simplified symbols . . . leaves us with a deep indefinable feeling of truth" (Orwell 1996, xviii–xix).

9. In his essay on fairy tales J. R. R. Tolkien does not mention *Animal Farm* and specifically excludes "beast-fables" from the category (1984, 117).

10. William Empson pointed out this aspect of *Animal Farm* to Orwell in a letter written not long after the book's publication: "the effect of the farmyard with its unescapable racial differences, is to suggest that the Russian scene had unescap-able social differences too—so the metaphor suggests that the Russian revolution was always a pathetically impossible attempt" (quoted in Crick 1989, 190).

11. In the essay on "Politics and Literature" (1946), however, Orwell refers to Jonathan Swift disparagingly as a "Tory anarchist," that is, someone who despises "authority while disbelieving in liberty" (1968a, 216).

12. That there is also some humor (and skepticism) here is indicated by the narrator's remark that the "stirring tune" to which "Beasts of England" was sung was "something between *Clementine* and *La Cucaracha*" (9).

13. Orwell is here satirizing the abolition of the "International" as the anthem of the Soviet Union in March 1944, when it was replaced by the "Song of Stalin." In the novel, the new anthem, composed by the pig Minimus, is called "Comrade Napoleon."

14. Either Orwell is forgetting here about the pigs' stealing the milk and the windfall apples or else the pigs are already undergoing their transformation from animals to humans and hence are no longer to he counted as fellow "animals."

15. In this connection it is worth remembering Orwell's remark in "In Front of Your Nose" (1946) that "the Russian people were taught for years that they were better off than anybody else, and propaganda posters showed Russian families sit-ting down to abundant meals while the proletariat of other countries starved in the gutter. Meanwhile the workers in the Western countries were so much better off

than those of the USSR that non-contact between Soviet citizens and outsiders had to be a guiding principle of policy" (1968a, 125).

16. Since it is often claimed that *Nineteen Eighty-Four* has little literary value, it is relevant to note here that the novelist Anthony Burgess admired *Nineteen Eighty-Four* so much that he not only wrote a kind of continuation-commentary, *1985*, but claimed to have read the novel thirty times (Aldiss 1984, 10).

17. Orwell reviewed the book for the *Tribune* in January 1946. In the review he argues, mistakenly I believe, that Aldous Huxley had read *We* and borrowed from it. Indisputable, however, is the debt that *Nineteen Eighty-Four* owes to Zamiatin's dsytopian novel. The betrayal by the narrator D-503 of his lover I-330 (prefiguring the betrayal of Julia by Winston) is among the most obvious similarities, if only because Orwell discusses it himself in his review (1968a, 74). According to George Steiner, "Without 'We,' 'Nineteen Eighty-Four,' in the guise in which we have it, simply would not exist" (1983, 174). For additional possible sources of the novel, see Rose (1992).

18. For Irving Howe the sex drive is the primary source of danger to the stability of the Oceanic state, though he implies that this is something that Orwell himself may not have been aware of. Howe reasons that if Winston and Julia's "needs as human beings force these two quite ordinary people to rebellion, may not the same thing happen to others?" (1971, 50).

19. See Chapter 5 of Firchow (1984) for a more extended discussion of the relation between *Nineteen Eighty-Four* and *Brave New World*.

20. Though some Western critics of *Nineteen Eighty-Four* (notably Raymond Williams, A. L. Rowse, and Scott Lucas) have attacked Orwell for betraying socialism, there was nothing like the vicious attack launched by the Soviet government, which denounced Orwell as "a former 'police agent and yellow correspondent' [journalist?] . . . who passes in England for a writer 'because there is a great demand for garbage there'" (quoted in Rodden 1988, 132). In this connection, it seems odd that even a relatively objective critic like Krishan Kumar claims that only "careless readers" of *Nineteen Eighty-Four* are given to identifying the world depicted in the novel with that of Stalin's Russia (Kumar 1993, 65).

21. It is true, however, as Brian Aldiss reminds us, that in his apartment O'Brien does enjoy some compensating comforts, which Winston can only marvel at: "There is wallpaper on the walls, the floors are carpeted, the telescreen can be switched off, the butler pours wine from a decanter, and there are good cigarettes in a silver box. Not sybaritic, exactly; more the sort of thing to which typical Old Etonians (Orwell was an untypical example) could be said to be accustomed" (1984, 9). Or, perhaps more to the point, these are the sorts of comforts and privileges which higher-ups in the Party came to expect as their due, as anyone who ever visited the former Soviet Union or its satellite states can testify.

22. Aldous Huxley pointed this out to Orwell in a letter thanking him for the gift of *Nineteen Eighty-Four*, saying: "Whether in actual fact the policy of the boot-on-the-face can go on indefinitely seems doubtful" (Huxley 1971, 102).

23. As is perhaps to be expected from someone with an almost professional interest in Marxism, Orwell may have been aware of Hegel's concept of the "end of history," though for him history appeared to be ending in a very un-Hegelian sense. In his 1943 essay on the war in Spain, Orwell remembered "saying once to Arthur Koestler, 'History stopped in 1936,' at which he nodded in immediate understanding." What the two friends were thinking about, Orwell claims, was not the triumph

of bourgeois, representative democracy but the systematic distortion of historical fact to the point where it was impossible to verify what had really happened—i.e., Winston's job at the ironically named Ministry of Truth. According to Bernard Crick, however, Orwell's knowledge of Marxist doctrine was less than complete, though he apparently was able to impress even orthodox Marxists with that knowledge (Crick 1980, 305). Though, like Crick, Werner von Koppenfels finds little evidence in Orwell of a profound knowledge of Marx's writings, he does cite a disguised allusion to the *Communist Manifesto* (in *The Road to Wigan Pier*) and points out that Orwell had a dog named Marx (1984, 660). William Steinhoff, on the other hand, claims that Orwell "knew a great deal about Marxism and he regarded Marx's theory as a 'useful instrument for testing other theories of thought'" (Steinhoff 1975, 73).

24. Orwell, in retrospect, was not particularly good at prophecy either. In "England Your England" (1941) he predicts that unless Britain loses the war against Germany the conclusion of hostilities "will wipe out most of the existing class privileges" (1954, 283). As William Steinhoff points out, Orwell also readily admitted that he had been wrong to predict Churchill's resignation after the disaster of the loss of Singapore to the Japanese in 1942 or, for that matter, the continued, long-term collaboration of Germany and the Soviet Union (1975, 102). In his two essays on James Burnham, Orwell faults Burnham for his inaccurate and frequently revised prophecies, though he does not mention his own flawed predictions in those contexts.

25. O'Brien's obviously Irish name is probably also intended to evoke associations with Catholicism and the Inquisition. According to Carl Freedman, Orwell's aversion for the Catholic Church was almost as intense as his hostility to the Soviet Union (1986, 98). As Crick also points out, "O'Brien's reference to the regime holding a Ptolemaic rather than Copernican cosmology must be intended to make us think of Galileo facing the papal inquisition and reveals a religiosity in O'Brien" (1989, 157). And according to William Steinhoff, Orwell had read Boris Souvarine's *Cauche-mar en U.R.S.S.*, which uses as its epigraph a quotation linking Galileo's submission to Church doctrine with the phony Moscow trial confessions (1975, 33). Orwell may also be thinking of the fanatic Irish Catholic villain of Joseph Conrad's *Romance*. His name is O'Brien. (At about the time Orwell was writing *Nineteen Eighty-Four* he was planning a long essay on Conrad which he did not live to complete.) O'Brien's link with Catholicism—and with Communism as well, of course—is especially evident in his compulsive need to have Winston make a full and genuinely contrite confession. Only then can Winston be absolved of his "sins," that is, when he sincerely expresses his love for Big Brother (i.e., God). It's worth noting in this connection, however, that O'Brien, the supposed devotee of "hatred," contradicts himself when he wants Winston's "treatment" to culminate in love. Or is this simply another manifestation of "doublethink"?

26. In "Writers and Leviathan" (1948) Orwell implicitly defines doublethink with reference to the alleged habit of the English Left to think of the word "socialism" as having the same meaning both in Russia and in England: "Hence there has arisen a sort of schizophrenic manner of thinking, in which words like 'democracy' can bear two irreconcilable meanings, and such things as concentration camps and mass deportations can be right and wrong simultaneously" (1968a, 410).

27. It's worth noting here that the vast effort expended at the Ministry of Truth to keep altering the past to conform with the currently expedient political facts makes very little sense in the context of the kind of police state Oceania is described as being. What citizen of this state, in his or her right mind, would dare

to examine the files of past newspapers in order to verify what had "actually" happened? Doing so would be an obvious invitation to the Thought Police to "examine" such a person more carefully in Room 101. In *Animal Farm*, however, the revision of the seven commandments by Squealer makes sense, since the animals are not hindered when they check the back of the barn to see what "new truth" the latest revision has brought them.

28. The assertion that forbidden thoughts cannot be expressed in Newspeak is not entirely accurate. For example, the Newspeak names of the various ministries— of love, peace, truth, and plenty—respectively, Miniluv, Minipax, Minitrue, and Miniplenty—strongly and ironically imply that they possess a "minimum" amount of love, peace, truth, and plenty. According to William Steinhoff, Orwell may have modeled Newspeak on the "cablese" that journalists used to write formerly when transmitting their copy to their editors via telegraph from overseas (1975, 169).

29. By now the telescreens have become synonymous with the idea of continuous surveillance, a feature of Orwell's state that contemporary Americans, especially, fear may be adopted by their own government. For Orwell the origins of this sort of universal surveillance are probably to be found in the universal spy mania prevalent in World War II but also relevant, if we are to believe Vita Fortunati (along with Michel Foucault), may be the so-called "panopticon," which permitted guards to keep a continual eye on prisoners in Jeremy Bentham's hypothetical prison (Fortunati 1987, 115).

30. It is suspicious that Julia disappears from the novel after the couple's apprehension by the Thought Police, only to reappear briefly when the two meet "by chance" and engage in a pointless conversation that makes Winston want to break off contact permanently. By this time Winston, to be sure, has found a new love interest in Big Brother. While it may be that Julia has indeed been subjected to torture in much the same way that Winston has been, there is no specific evidence for it; and, given the skill with which O'Brien and his cohorts contrive to disguise people (e.g., Charrington), it's perhaps justifiable to speculate that Julia's new appearance may simply be another development in O'Brien's "subtle" drama. Another small piece of evidence suggesting that Julia may be O'Brien's stooge is her failure to react when Winston tells her that he recognizes the details of the landscape of the Golden Country because he has seen it before "sometimes in a dream" (109).

31. I, for one, strongly sympathize with the long tradition of Orwell criticism, including such distinguished figures as George Kateb and Irving Howe, that shares Morris Dickstein's view about O'Brien, namely, that "he may embody the system but he cannot plausibly speak for it. O'Brien is no Grand Inquisitor, whose arguments he tries to match." The earlier critics differ, however, from Dickstein by taking O'Brien's mania seriously, or, rather, by not supporting Dickstein's claims that Orwell means us to think of O'Brien as relatively normal, since in his view "the book offers little support for seeing this thuggish creature as a madman who plays mind games with his victims" (2004, 65). Dickstein also shows no awareness of the existence of the double plot in *Nineteen Eighty-Four*, though Thomas Pynchon apparently does in his introduction to a recent edition of *Nineteen Eighty-Four* (Deery 2005, 123). (I pointed out its existence as long ago as 1984 in the concluding chapter of my *End of Utopia*.) That O'Brien's lust for power is psychologically unmotivated was noted as early as 1949 by Philip Rahv in his review of *Nineteen Eighty-Four*, when he said that even Dostoyevsky's Grand Inquisitor felt the need to justify his exercise of arbitrary power, whereas O'Brien does not. Irving Howe,

after quoting Rahv, argues that Orwell is depicting a totalitarian society that has reached a stage "when belief in the total state is crumbling while its power survives" (Howe 1983, 12–13). The absence of any justifying ideology is also problematic for George Kateb, who, in what is probably the best discussion of this important aspect of the novel, faults Orwell for failing to explain why men like O'Brien want power. In his view Orwell, like Winston, seems to know a great deal about the "how" but not much about the "why" of the power motive (Kateb 1971, 82–87).

32. The most thorough discussion of the relation of the Appendix to the story of Winston Smith is Richard Sanderson's 1988 essay, which argues that there is no way of telling if the Appendix is told by a different narrative voice from the one in *Nineteen Eighty-Four*. In his view, one should therefore not take into account "the essay's clues" as reliable indications of "the future downfall of Big Brother." Sanderson also professes to be puzzled as to why Orwell would have signaled the demise of Oceania in so indirect and ambiguous a fashion if he really meant to leave his readers with the sense of a happy ending (589–90). By way of an answer, one might point out that Orwell after all was a literary artist and not a mere propagandist, and that, as such, he had a right to expect his readers to extrapolate from the evidence he provided, including the evidence of the covert plot in the novel proper—something that Sanderson seems to be unaware of.

33. William Casement is one of the few critics of the novel who shares, though with qualifications, some of Winston's hope in the possibility of the proles bringing about the destruction of Oceania (1989, 219).

34. As William Steinhoff points out, Orwell's use of the "2 + 2 = 5" formula is derived from the first Soviet five-year plan, which was supposed to be completed in four rather than five years (1975, 172). While the placement of such an apparently absurd notion in a historical context makes it appear rational—and therefore may make O'Brien seem rational too—few readers of *Nineteen Eighty-Four* would have caught the allusion, and even if they had, they might have missed the irony in Orwell's reference to a propagandistic plan which had not succeeded either in four or even in five years.

35. Additional evidence that Orwell must have meant his readers to treat O'Brien's claims skeptically is to be found in his essay "James Burnham and the Managerial Revolution" (1946), which he wrote after he had already begun work on *Nineteen Eighty-Four*. In that essay Orwell wonders why Burnham, who, like O'Brien, is obsessed with power, "never stops to ask *why* people want power. He seems to assume that power hunger, although only dominant in comparatively few people, is a natural instinct that does not have to be explained, like the desire for food" (1968a, 177). Later in the essay, Orwell goes on to question Burnham's claim that "literally anything can become right or wrong if the dominant class wills it." Not so, says Orwell, because Burnham "ignores the fact that certain rules of conduct have to be observed if human society is to hold together at all." Orwell then goes on to speculate that Russian policy will probably lead to atomic war, but even if it doesn't, "the Russian regime will either democratise itself or it will perish. The huge, invincible, everlasting ["Forever!"] empire of which Burnham appears to dream will not be established, or, if established, will not endure, because slavery is no longer a stable basis for human society" (180). Are we to suppose from this evidence that Orwell made one prediction about the future of totalitarianism in the essay on Burnham and another, utterly different one, in the approximately contemporaneous *Nineteen Eighty-Four*? It's possible, of course, but I'm inclined to doubt it.

Chronology

1903	Eric Arthur Blair (later to become George Orwell) is born June 25 in Bengal, India, to a middle-class English family that is connected to the British colonial administration in India and Burma.
1907	Moves to England with his mother and sister.
1911–16	Schooled at St. Cyprian's.
1917–21	Attends Eton on scholarship.
1922–27	Serves with Indian Imperial Police in Burma.
1928–29	In Paris, works as dishwasher and writer; first articles published in newspapers.
1930–34	Lives mainly in London. Publishes articles and translations. *Down and Out in Paris and London* published in 1933 under pen name George Orwell. In 1934, *Burmese Days* is published.
1935	*A Clergyman's Daughter* is published.
1936	*Keep the Aspidistra Flying* is published. Marries Eileen O'Shaughnessy. Leaves for Spain in December to join anti-Fascists in Barcelona. Serves four months on the Aragon Front.
1937	*The Road to Wigan Pier* is published. Wounded in the throat, returns to England.

1938	*Homage to Catalonia* is published. Spends several months in a sanitarium to treat his tuberculosis, then visits Morocco for the winter.
1939	*Coming Up for Air* is published.
1940–43	Publishes *"Inside the Whale" and Other Essays* in 1940. Medically unfit for service in World War II, joins the Home Guard in London. Writes and broadcasts as wartime propagandist for the BBC. In 1941, publishes *The Lion and the Unicorn: Socialism and the English Genius.* In 1943, becomes literary editor of the *Tribune*.
1944	Adopts a son, whom he names Richard Horatio Blair.
1945	Correspondent for *The Observer*. His wife dies. *Animal Farm* is published.
1946	Publishes *Critical Essays: Dickens, Dali, and Others.* Rents house in the Hebrides.
1947–48	Hospitalized for seven months, starting in December, for tuberculosis.
1949	Publishes *1984*. Marries Sonia Brownell; health continues to decline.
1950	Dies of tuberculosis on January 21. *"Shooting an Elephant" and Other Essays* is published.
1953	*"England, Your England" and Other Essays* is published.
1961	*Collected Essays* is published.

Contributors

HAROLD BLOOM is Sterling Professor of the Humanities at Yale University. He is the author of 30 books, including *Shelley's Mythmaking, The Visionary Company, Blake's Apocalypse, Yeats, A Map of Misreading, Kabbalah and Criticism, Agon: Toward a Theory of Revisionism, The American Religion, The Western Canon,* and *Omens of Millennium: The Gnosis of Angels, Dreams, and Resurrection. The Anxiety of Influence* sets forth Professor Bloom's provocative theory of the literary relationships between the great writers and their predecessors. His most recent books include *Shakespeare: The Invention of the Human,* a 1998 National Book Award finalist, *How to Read and Why, Genius: A Mosaic of One Hundred Exemplary Creative Minds, Hamlet: Poem Unlimited, Where Shall Wisdom Be Found?,* and *Jesus and Yahweh: The Names Divine.* In 1999, Professor Bloom received the prestigious American Academy of Arts and Letters Gold Medal for Criticism. He has also received the International Prize of Catalonia, the Alfonso Reyes Prize of Mexico, and the Hans Christian Andersen Bicentennial Prize of Denmark.

DAPHNE PATAI is a professor at the University of Massachusetts at Amherst. In addition to her book on Orwell, she has published *Looking Backward, 1988–1888: Essays on Edward Bellamy.*

VALERIE MEYERS is the author of *George Orwell,* part of St. Martin's Modern Novelists series, and co-author of *George Orwell: An Annotated Bibliography of Criticism.*

SAMIR ELBARBARY is affiliated with Kuwait University. In addition to his work on Orwell, he has written on Joseph Conrad, D.H. Lawrence, Thomas Hardy, and James Joyce.

V.C. LETEMENDIA has written *Free from Hunger and the Whip: Exploring the Political Development of George Orwell* and also has written on Sartre.

ROGER FOWLER was a professor and the first dean of the School at the University of East Anglia in Norwich, United Kingdom. He was a pioneer in critical linguistics and authored *Linguistic Criticism* as well as a book on Orwell.

ROBERT PEARCE was a professor of history at the University College of St. Martin, Lancaster, a fellow of the Royal Historical Society, and the author of a dozen history books.

ANTHONY STEWART is an associate professor of English at Dalhousie University, Halifax, Nova Scotia. His teaching and research areas include Orwell, Anglo-American modernism, and the contemporary African-American essay.

PETER EDGERLY FIRCHOW was professor emeritus of English at the University of Minnesota, where he was a member of the department for 40 years. He was the author of *The End of Utopia: A Study of Aldous Huxley's Brave New World* and additional works on Conrad, Auden, and others.

Bibliography

Alldritt, Keith. *The Making of George Orwell: An Essay in Literary History*. New York: St. Martin's Press, 1961.

Bowker, Gordon. *Inside George Orwell*. New York: Palgrave Macmillan, 2003.

Cushman, Thomas, and John Rodden, eds. *George Orwell: Into the Twenty-first Century*. Boulder, Colo.: Paradigm, 2004.

Fenwick, Gillian. *George Orwell: A Bibliography*. New Castle, Del.: Oak Knoll, 1998.

Fergenson, Laraine. "George Orwell's *Animal Farm*: A Twentieth-Century Beast Fable." *Bestia: Yearbook of the Beast Fable Society* 2 (May 1990): 109–18.

Fishelov, David. "Satura Contra Utopiam: Satirical Distortions of Utopian Ideas." *Revue de Litterature Comparee* 67, no. 4 (October–December 1993): 463–71.

Ford, Boris, ed. *From Orwell to Naipaul*. London: Penguin, 1995.

Gottlieb, Erika. *The Orwell Conundrum: A Cry of Despair or Faith in the Spirit of Man?* Ottawa: Carleton University Press, 1992.

———. "George Orwell's Dystopias: *Animal Farm* and *Nineteen Eighty-Four*." In *A Companion to the British and Irish Novel, 1945–2000*, edited by Brian W. Shaffer, pp. 241–53. Malden, Mass.: Blackwell, 2005.

Greenblatt, Stephen Jay. *Three Modern Satirists: Waugh, Orwell, and Huxley*. New Haven: Yale University Press, 1965.

Grofman, Bernard. "Pig and Proletariat: *Animal Farm* as History." *San José Studies* 16, no. 2 (Spring 1990): 5–39.

Gross, Miriam. *The World of George Orwell*. London: Weidenfield & Nicholson, 1971.

Hitchens, Christopher. *Orwell's Victory*. London; New York: Allen Lane/Penguin Press, 2002.

————. *Why Orwell Matters*. New York: Basic Books, 2002.

Holderness, Graham, Bryan Loughrey, and Nahem Yousaf. *George Orwell*. New York, N.Y.: St. Martin's, 1998.

Hollis, Christopher. *A Study of George Orwell*. London: Hollis and Carter, 1956.

Kerr, Douglas. "Colonial Habits: Orwell and Woolf in the Jungle." *English Studies* 78, no. 12 (March 1997): 149–61.

————. "Orwell, Animals, and the East." *Essays in Criticism* 49, no. 3 (July 1999): 234–55.

Leab, Daniel J. *Orwell Subverted: The CIA and the Filming of* Animal Farm. University Park: Pennsylvania State University Press, 2007.

Lee, Robert A. "The Uses of Form: A Reading of *Animal Farm*." *Studies in Short Fiction* 6 (1969): 557–73.

Meyers, Jeffrey. "Orwell's Bestiary: The Political Allegory of *Animal Farm*." *Studies in the Twentieth Century* 8 (1971): 65–84.

————. "George Orwell and the Art of Writing." *Kenyon Review* 27, no. 4 (Fall 2005): 92–114.

Meyers, Jeffrey, ed. *George Orwell: The Critical Heritage*. London; New York: Routledge, 1975.

Mezciems, Jenny. "Swift and Orwell: Utopia as Nightmare." In *Between Dream and Nature: Essays on Utopia and Dystopia*, edited by Dominic Baker-Smith and C. C. Barfoot, pp. 91–112. Amsterdam: Rodopi, 1987.

Morse, Donald E. "'A Blatancy of Untruth': George Orwell's Uses of the Fantastic in *Animal Farm*." *Hungarian Journal of English and American Studies* 1, no. 2 (1995): 85–92.

Newsinger, John. *Orwell's Politics*. New York; London: St. Martin's Press; Macmillan Press, 1999.

O'Neill, Terry, ed. *Readings on* Animal Farm. San Diego, Calif.: Greenhaven, 1998.

Paden, Frances Freeman. "Narrative Dynamics in *Animal Farm*." *Literature in Performance: A Journal of Literary and Performing Art* 5, no. 2 (April 1985): 49–55.

Rodden, John. "Soviet Literary Policy, 1945–1989: The Case of George Orwell." *Modern Age* 32, no. 2 (Spring 1988): 131–39.

————. *The Politics of Literary Reputation: The Making and Claiming of "St. George" Orwell*. Oxford: Oxford University Press, 1989.

————. "Appreciating *Animal Farm* in the New Millennium." *Modern Age* 45, no. 1 (2003): 67–76.

Rosi, John. "Orwell and Patriotism." *Contemporary Review* 261, no. 1519 (August 1992): 95–100.

Savage, Robert. "Are Rats Comrades? Some Readings of a Question in George Orwell." *Colloquy: Text Theory Critique* 12 (November 2006): 83–90.

Schakel, Peter J. "That 'Hideous Strength' in Lewis and Orwell: A Comparison and Contrast." *Mythlore: A Journal of J. R. R. Tolkien, C. S. Lewis, Charles Williams, and the Genres of Myth and Fantasy Studies* 13, no. 4 (Summer 1987): 36–40.

Sedley, Stephen. "An Immodest Proposal: *Animal Farm*." In *Inside the Myth: Orwell: Views from the Left*, edited by Christopher Norris. London: Lawrence & Wishart, 1982.

Sewiall, Harry. "George Orwell's *Animal Farm*: A Metonym for a Dictatorship." *Journal of Literary Criticism, Comparative Linguistics, and Literary Studies* 23, no. 3 (November 2002): 81–96.

Taylor, D. J. *Orwell: The Life*. New York: Henry Holt & Co., 2003.

Todorov, Tzvetan. "Politics, Morality, and the Writer's Life: Notes on George Orwell." *Stanford French Review* 16, no. 1 (1992): 136–42.

Warburg, Fredric. "*Animal Farm* and *1984*." In *All Authors Are Equal*. London: Hutchinson, 1973; New York: St. Martin's Press, 1974.

Williams, Raymond. *George Orwell: A Collection of Critical Essays*. Englewood Cliffs, N.J.: Prentice-Hall, 1974.

———. *Orwell*. London: Fontana, 1991.

Wilson, Brendan. "Satire and Subversion: Orwell and the Uses of Anti-Climax." *Connotations: A Journal for Critical Debate* 4, no. 3 (1994–1995): 207–224.

Woodcock, George. *The Crystal Spirit: A Study of George Orwell*. Boston: Little, Brown, 1966.

Zwerdling, Alex. *Orwell and the Left*. New Haven: Yale University Press, 1974.

Acknowledgments

Daphne Patai, "Political Fiction and Patriarchal Fantasy." From *The Orwell Mystique: A Study in Male Ideology.* © 1984 by Daphne Patai and published by the University of Massachusetts Press.

Valerie Myers, *"Animal Farm:* An Allegory of Revolution." From *Modern Novelists: George Orwell*, St. Martin's Press. © 1991 by Valerie Meyers. Reprinted with permission of Palgrave Macmillan.

Samir Elbarbary, "Language as Theme in *Animal Farm.*" From *The International Fiction Review* 19, no. 1 (1992): 31–38. © 1992 by International Fiction Association.

V.C. Letemendia, "Revolution on *Animal Farm:* Orwell's Neglected Commentary." From *Journal of Modern Literature* 18, no. 1 (Winter 1992): 127–37. © 1992 by Indiana University Press. Reprinted by permission.

Roger Fowler, *"Animal Farm."* From *The Language of George Orwell*, St. Martin's Press. © 1995 by Roger Fowler. Reprinted with permission of Palgrave Macmillan.

Robert Pearce, "Orwell, Tolstoy, and *Animal Farm*" by Robert Pearce. From *The Review of English Studies,* New Series, 49, no. 193 (February 1998): 64–69. © 1998 by Oxford University Press.

Anthony Stewart, "An Absence of Pampering: The Betrayal of the Rebellion and the End of Decency in *Animal Farm*." From *George Orwell, Doubleness, and the Value of Decency*. © 2003 by Taylor & Francis Group LLC—Books. Reproduced with permission of Taylor & Francis Group LLC—Books in the format other book via Copyright Clearance Center.

Peter Edgerly Firchow, "George Orwell's Dystopias: From *Animal Farm* to *Nineteen Eighty-Four*." From *Modern Utopian Fictions: From H. G. Wells to Iris Murdoch*. © 2007 by the Catholic University of America Press. Used with permission: The Catholic University of America Press, Washington, DC.

Index

Characters in literary works are indexed by first name (if any), followed by the name of the work in parentheses